KB271484

초등
영단어
따라쓰기
A G m P W 6

초등영단어 따라쓰기

초판 1쇄 펴낸날 2013년 1월 20일
초판 8쇄 펴낸날 2020년 12월 10일

지은이 정희경
펴낸이 배태수 ___**펴낸곳** 신라출판사
등 록 1975년 5월 23일 제6-0216호
전 화 02)922-4735 ___**팩 스** 02)6935-1285
주 소 구로구 중앙로 3길12 서봉빌딩
북 디자인 디자인 디도

ISBN 978-89-7244-118-2 13740
*잘못된 책은 구입한 곳에서 바꾸어 드립니다.

초등 영단어 따라쓰기

정희경 엮음

신라출판사

머리말

오늘날 우리들은 세계화 속에서 살고 있으며, 영어는 세계 공용어로서 문화의 벽을 넘어 의사소통의 수단으로서 일상생활에서 반드시 필요한 언어가 되었습니다. 우리들이 외국 여행을 할 때 또 각 나라에서 국내로 들어오는 여행객들의 숫자 또한 예전과는 비교할 수 없을 정도로 많아졌습니다. 또한 업무처리의 의사소통 수단으로서 영어를 쓰고 있으며, 거리마다 넘쳐나는 유학생, 관광객 등을 자주 만나게 됩니다.

외국어를 익히기에 가장 적절한 때는 초등학교 전후부터 시작하는 것이 모국어와 같이 자연스럽게 배울 수 있어서 적합하다고 합니다. 그런데 그 시작은 단어를 먼저 배우는 것이 유리하다고 합니다. 단어만 알고 있다고 어떤 것이나 의미가 통한다는 뜻은 아니지만 단어를 알지 못하고는 의사를 전달할 수도, 받을 수도 없습니다. 영어란 단어와 단어의 연결이므로 필요한 단어를 모르면 어찌할 도리가 없는 것입니다.

이 책에서는 초등학생이 영어 기초를 확실히 잡을 수 있도록 꼭 알아야 할 필수 영단어와 중학교 초급단계에서 익혀야 할 1080단어를 알파벳 순서대로 배열하였습니다. 또한 빠르고 효율적으로 익힐 수 있도록 발음기호와 영어발음을 한글로 함께 표기하고 단어에 맞는 예쁜 그림을 알맞게 배열하여 재미를 갖도록 구성하였으며 단어를 눈으로 보고. 입으로 말하고, 손으로 선 위에 따라 쓰면서 암기와 함께 쓰기를 배울 수 있도록 꾸몄습니다. 아무쪼록 영단어 따라 쓰기가 어린이 여러분의 영어 기초를 확실히 잡을 수 있기를 바랍니다.

엮은이

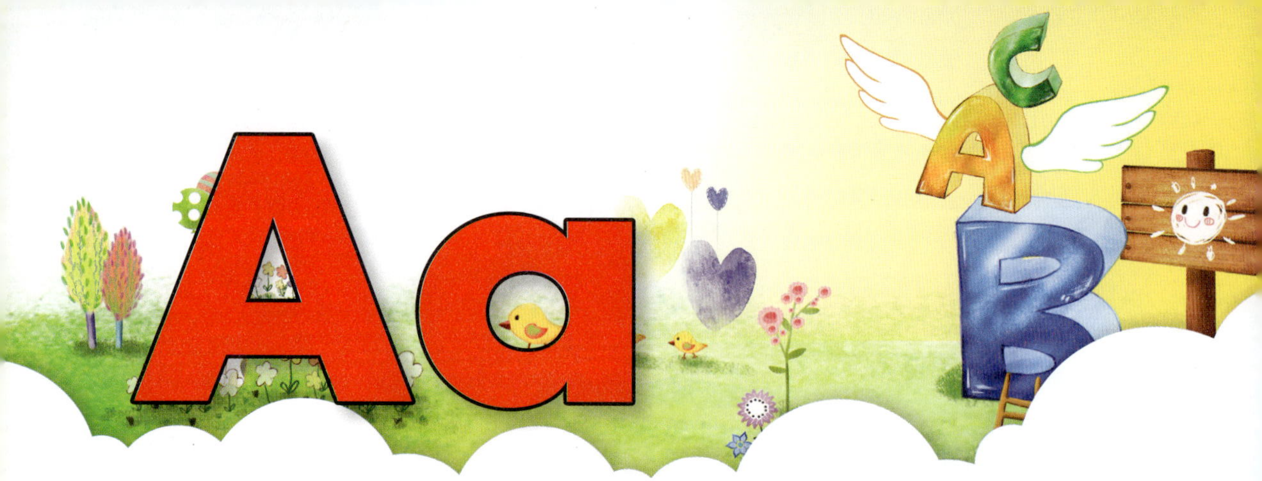

Aa

a
[ə 어]
관 하나의(자음 앞)

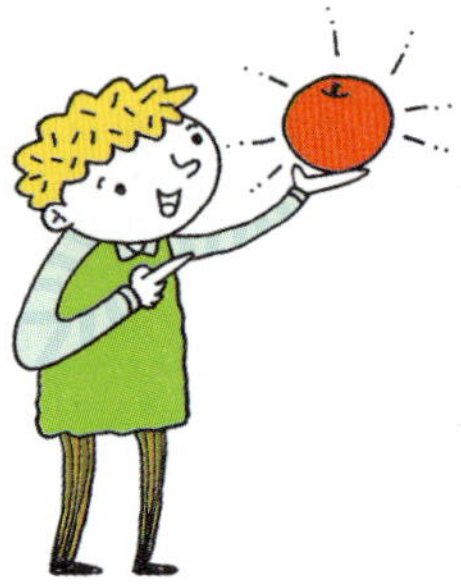

a

about
[əbáut 어바우트]
전 ~에 대하여, 약

about about about about about

across
[əkrɔ́ːs 어크로-스]
전 건너편에

across across across

act

[ækt 액트]
동 행동하다

act　act　act　act

address

[ədrés 어드레스]
명 주소

address　address　address　address

afraid

[əfréid 어프레이드]
형 무서워하는

afraid　afraid　afraid

after

[æftər 애프터]
전 ～의 뒤에

after　after　after　after　after　after

afternoon
[ǽftərnúːn 애프터누-운]
명 오후

afternoon   afternoon

again
[əgéin 어게인]
부 다시, 또

again   again   again   again   again

age
[eidʒ 에이쥐]
명 나이

age   age   age   age

ago
[əgóu 어고우]
부 ~전에

ago   ago   ago   ago   ago   ago

agree

[əgríː 어그리–]
동 동의하다, 생각이 같다

agree   agree   agree

air

[ɛər 에어]
명 공기

air   air   air   air   air   air   air

airplane

[ɛ́ərplèin 에어플레인]
명 비행기

airplane   airplane

airport

[ɛ́ərpɔ̀ːrt 에어포–트]
명 비행장

airport   airport   airport   airport

album

[ǽlbəm 앨범]
명 앨범

album　album　album　album　album

all

[ɔːl 오-올]
형 모든, 전부의

all　all　all　all　all

almost

[ɔ́ːlmoust 오-올모우스트]
부 거의, 대부분

almost　almost　almost　almost

along

[əlɔ́ːŋ 얼로-옹]
전 ～을 따라

along　along　along

alphabet

[ǽlfəbèt 앨퍼벳]
명 알파벳, 자모

alphabet　alphabet

already

[ɔːlrédi 오-올레디]
부 이미, 벌써

already　already

also

[ɔ́ːlsou 오-올소우]
부 ～도 또한

also　also　also　also　also　also

always

[ɔ́ːlweiz 오-올웨이즈]
부 언제나, 항상

always　always　always　always

ambulance [ǽmbjuləns 앰뷸런스]
명 구급차

ambulance ambulance ambulance

among [əmʌ́ŋ 어망]
전 ～의 사이에(서)

among among

and [ǽnd 앤드]
접 ～와/과, 그리고

and and and and and and

angry [ǽŋgri 앵그리]
형 화난

angry angry angry

animal

[ǽnəməl 애너멀]
명 동물

animal　　　animal

another

[ənʌ́ðər 어나더]
형 다른 하나의, 다른

another　another　another　another

answer

[ǽnsər 앤서]
명 동 대답(하다)

answer　　answer

any

[éni 에니]
형 무언가의, 조금도

any　any　any　any　any　any　any

apartment

[əpáːrtmənt 어파–트먼트]
명 아파트

apartment apartment apartment

apple

[ǽpl 애플]
명 사과

apple apple apple

April

[éiprəl 에이프릴]
명 4월

April April April April April

apron

[éiprən 에이프런]
명 앞치마

apron apron apron

around [əráund 어라운드]
부 주위에, 여기저기에

around　around

arrive [əráiv 어라이브]
동 도착하다

arrive　arrive　arrive　arrive　arrive

August [ɔ́:gəst 오-거스트]
명 8월

August　August　August　August

aunt [ænt 앤트]
명 아주머니, 숙모, 이(고)모

aunt aunt aunt aunt

autumn

[ɔ́:təm 오-텀]
명 가을

autumn autumn autumn autumn

away

[əwéi 어웨이]
부 떨어져서, 저쪽으로

away away away

Bb

baby [béibi 베이비]
명 갓난아이

baby baby baby baby baby

back [bæk 백]
부 뒤에

back back back back back

bad [bæd 뱃]
형 나쁜

bad bad bad bad

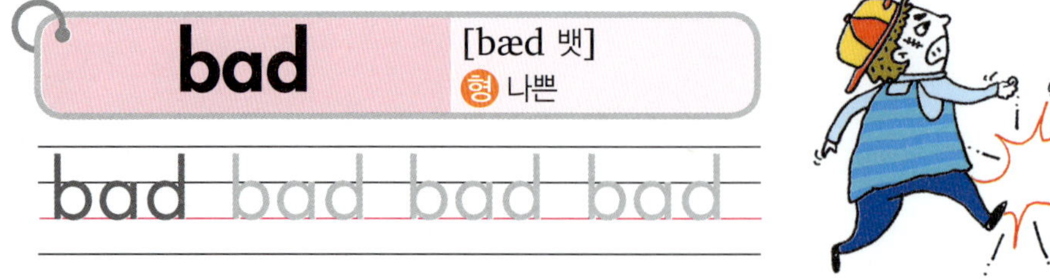

bag
[bæg 백]
명 (손)가방

bag　　bag　　bag　　bag　　bag　　bag

ball
[bɔːl 보-올]
명 공

ball　　ball　　ball　　ball

balloon
[bəlúːn 벌루-운]
명 풍선

balloon　　balloon

banana
[bənǽnə 버내너]
명 바나나

banana　banana　banana　banana

band

[bænd 밴드]
명 악대, 악단

band   band   band   band   band

bank

[bæŋk 뱅크]
명 은행.

bank   bank   bank

barber

[báːrbər 바-버]
명 이발사

barber   barber

baseball

[béisbɔ̀ːl 베이스보-올]
명 야구

baseball   baseball   baseball

basket

[bǽskit 배스킷]
(명) 바구니

basket　　basket　　basket　　basket

bath

[bæθ 배쓰]
(명) 목욕, 목욕통

bath　　bath　　bath

bathroom

[bǽθrù(:)m 배쓰룸]
(명) 욕실; 화장실

bathroom　　bathroom　　bathroom

beach

[bi:tʃ 비-취]
(명) 해변, 물가

beach beach beach

bear

[bɛər 베어]
명 곰.

bear　　bear　　bear

beautiful

[bjú:təfəl 뷰-터펄]
형 아름다운

beautiful　　beautiful　　beautiful

because

[bikɔ́:z 비코-즈]
접 ～ 때문에

because　　because

become

[bikʌ́m 비컴]
동 ～이 되다.

become　　become　　become

bed

[bed 벳]
명 침대

bed   bed   bed   bed

bedroom

[bédrù:m 베드루-움]
명 침실

bedroom   bedroom   bedroom

bee

[bi: 비-]
명 꿀벌

bee   bee   bee   bee

before

[bifɔ́:r 비포-]
전 ~앞에

before   before   before   before

begin

[bigín 비긴]
동 시작하다

begin begin begin begin begin

behind

[biháind 비하인드]
부 ~뒤에

behind behind behind behind

bell

[bel 벨]
명 종, 초인종

bell bell bell bell

below

[bilóu 빌로우]
전 ~의 아래에

below below below below

belt

[belt 벨트]
명 띠, 벨트

belt   belt   belt   belt   belt   belt

bench

[bentʃ 벤취]
명 긴 의자

bench   bench   bench

beside

[bisáid 비사이드]
전 ~의 옆에

beside   beside

best

[best 베스트]
형 가장 좋은

best   best   best   best   best   best

better

[bétər 베터]
형 ~보다 좋은

better better better better better

between

[bitwí:n 비튀-인]
전 ~의 사이에

between between

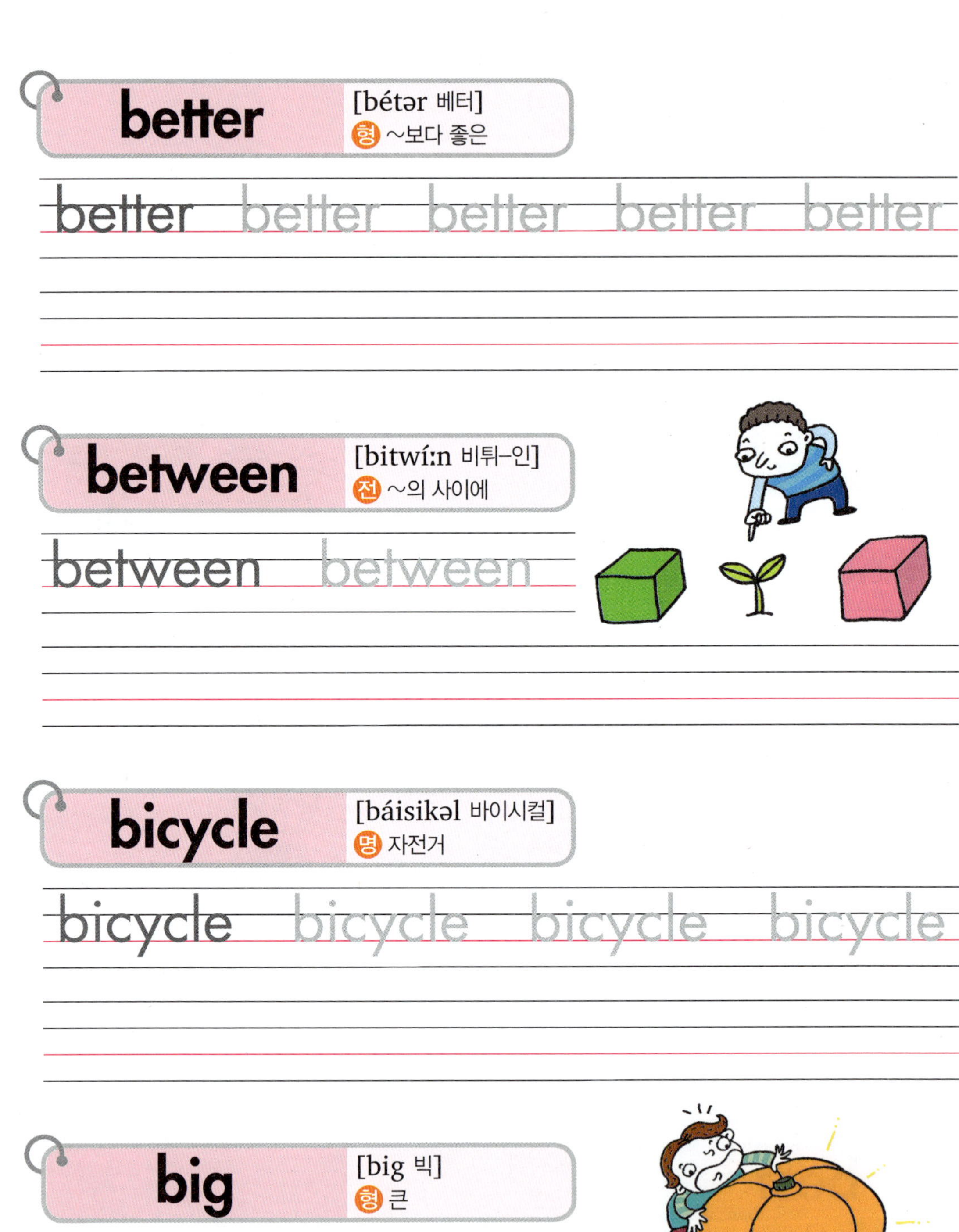

bicycle

[báisikəl 바이시컬]
명 자전거

bicycle bicycle bicycle bicycle

big

[big 빅]
형 큰

big big big big

bill

[bil 빌]
명 계산서

bill bill bill bill bill bill bill

bike

[baik 바이크]
명 자전거

bike bike bike bike

bird

[bə:rd 버-드]
명 새

bird bird bird bird

birthday

[bə́:rəðèi 버-쓰데이]
명 생일

birthday birthday birthday

black

[blæk 블랙]
형 검은

black　black　black　black　black

blackboard

[blǽkbɔ̀:rd 블랙보–드]
명 칠판.

blackboard blackboard blackboard

blind

[blaind 블라인드]
형 장님의

blind　blind　blind

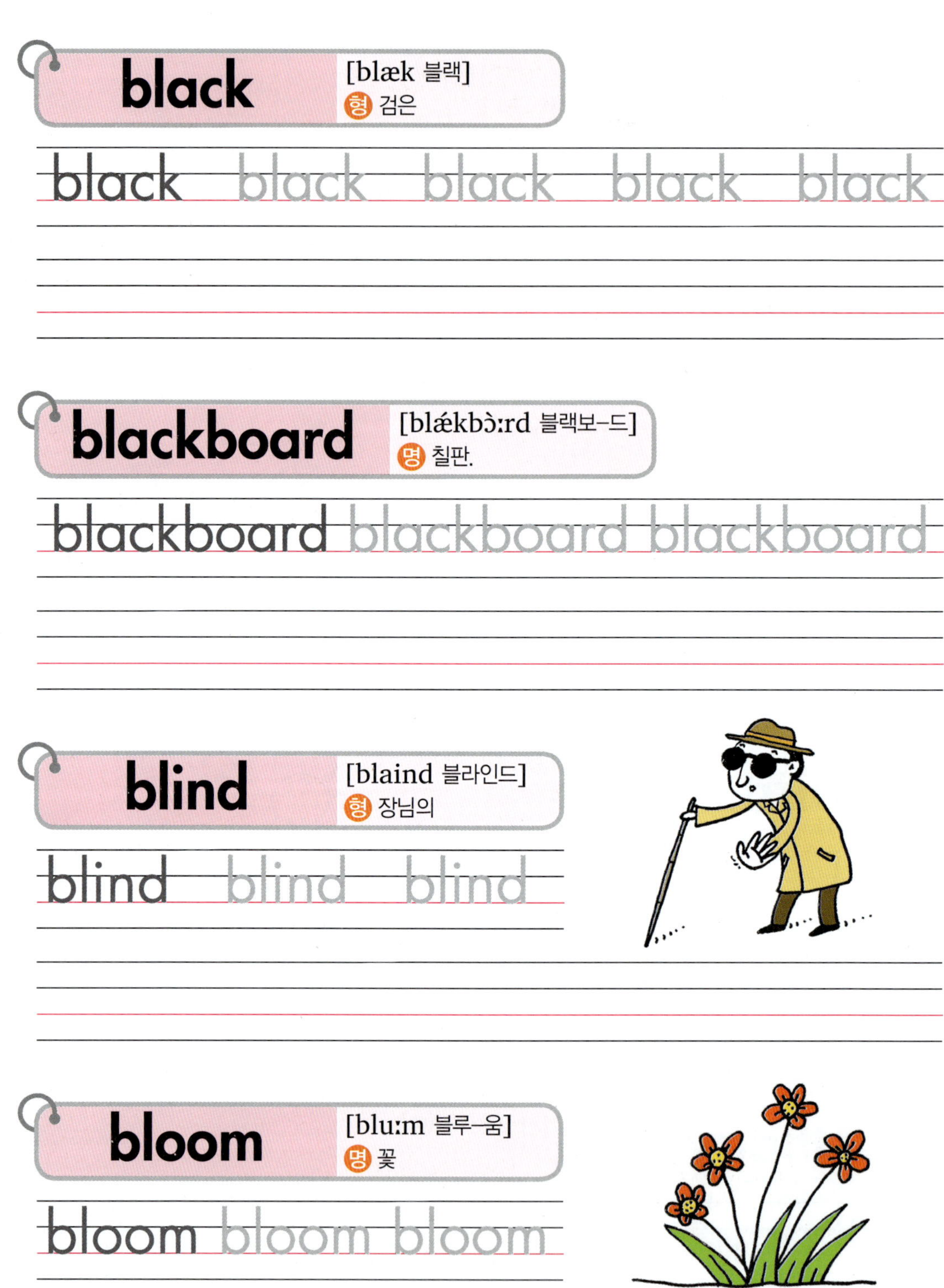

bloom

[blu:m 블루–움]
명 꽃

bloom bloom bloom

blow
[blou 블로우]
동 (바람이)불다

blow　blow　blow

blue
[bluː 블루-]
형 푸른, 하늘빛의

blue　blue　blue　blue　blue　blue

board
[bɔːrd 보-드]
명 게시판, 널빤지

board　board　board　board

boast
[boust 보우스트]
동 자랑하다

boast　boast　boast

boat

[bout 보우트]
명 보트, 작은 배

boat   boat   boat   boat   boat   boat

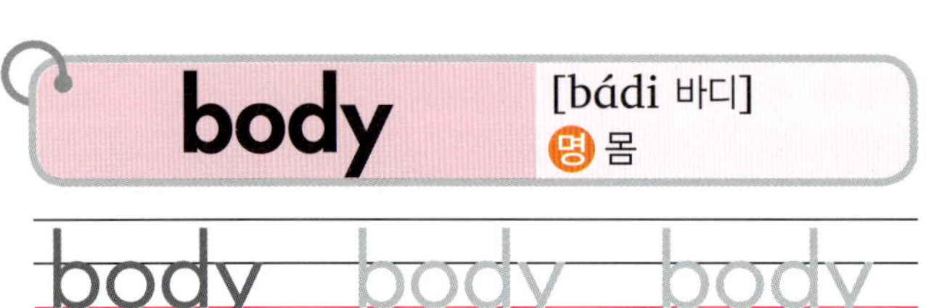

body

[bádi 바디]
명 몸

body   body   body

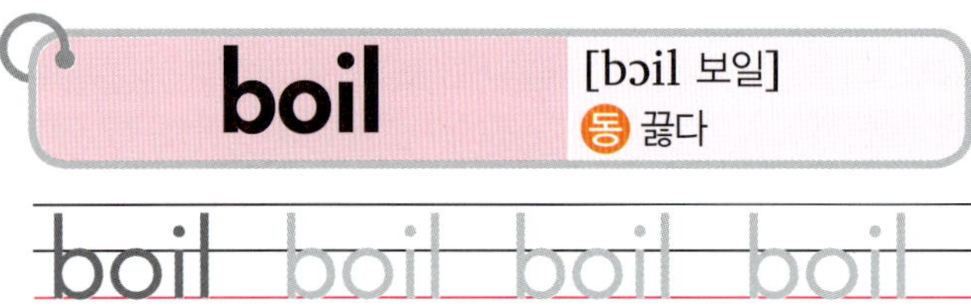

boil

[bɔil 보일]
동 끓다

boil   boil   boil   boil

bone

[boun 보운]
명 뼈

bone   bone   bone   bone   bone

book

[buk 북]
명 책

book   book   book

bookshelf

[búkʃèlf 북쉘프]
명 책꽂이

bookshelf   bookshelf   bookshelf

bookstore

[búkstɔ̀ːr 북스토-]
명 책방, 서점

bookstore   bookstore   bookstore

boot

[buːt 부-트]
명 장화, 부츠

boot boot boot boot boot boot

born

[bɔːrn 보-온]
형 타고난

born born born born born born

borrow

[bɔ́rou 보로우]
동 빌리다, 돈을 꾸다

borrow borrow

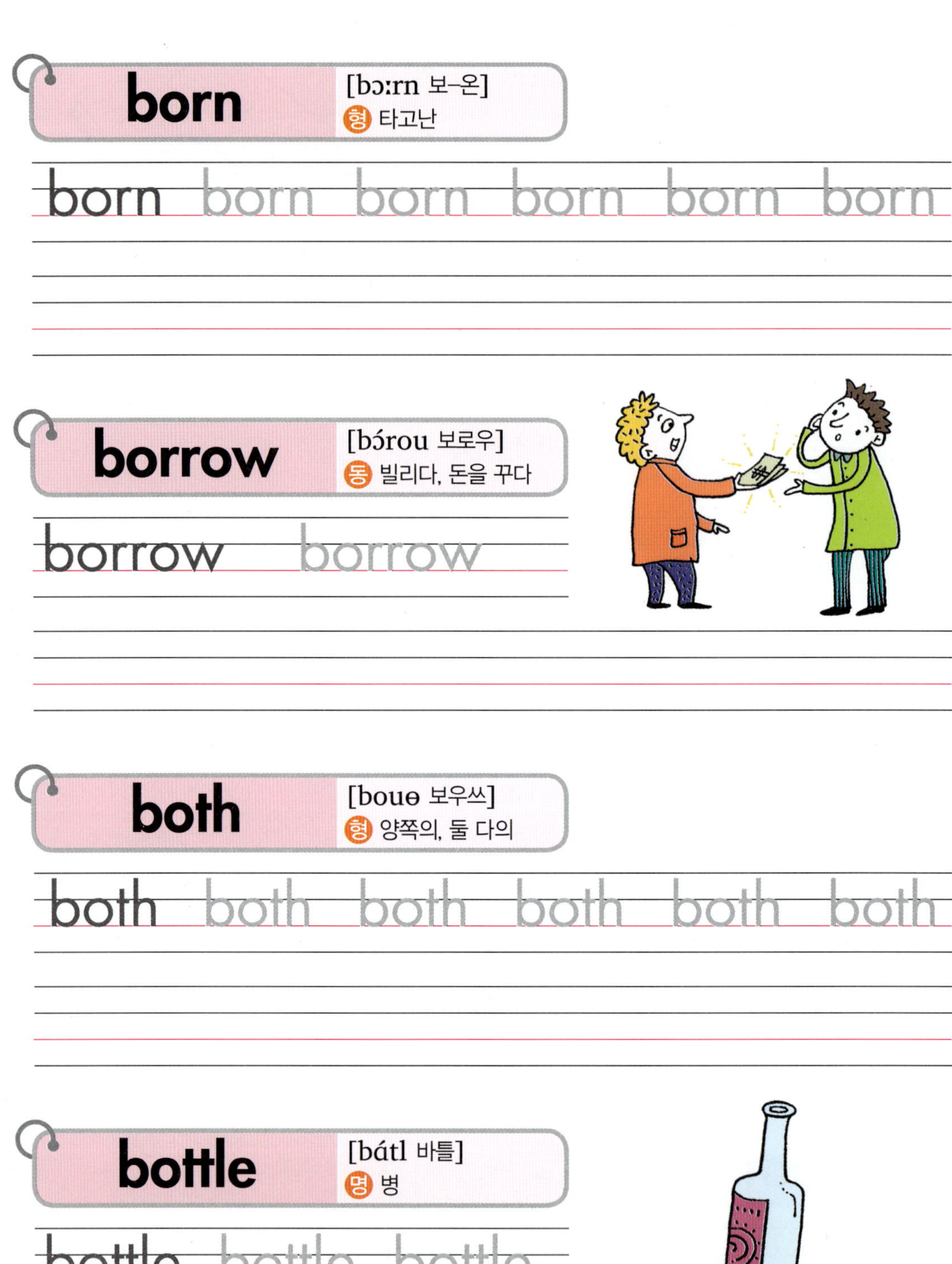

both

[bouθ 보우쓰]
형 양쪽의, 둘 다의

both both both both both both

bottle

[bǽtl 바틀]
명 병

bottle bottle bottle

bottom

[bátəm 바텀]
명 밑바닥

bottom bottom bottom bottom

bow

[bau 바우]
동 절하다

bow bow bow bow bow

bowl

[boul 보울]
명 사발, 공기

bowl bowl bowl

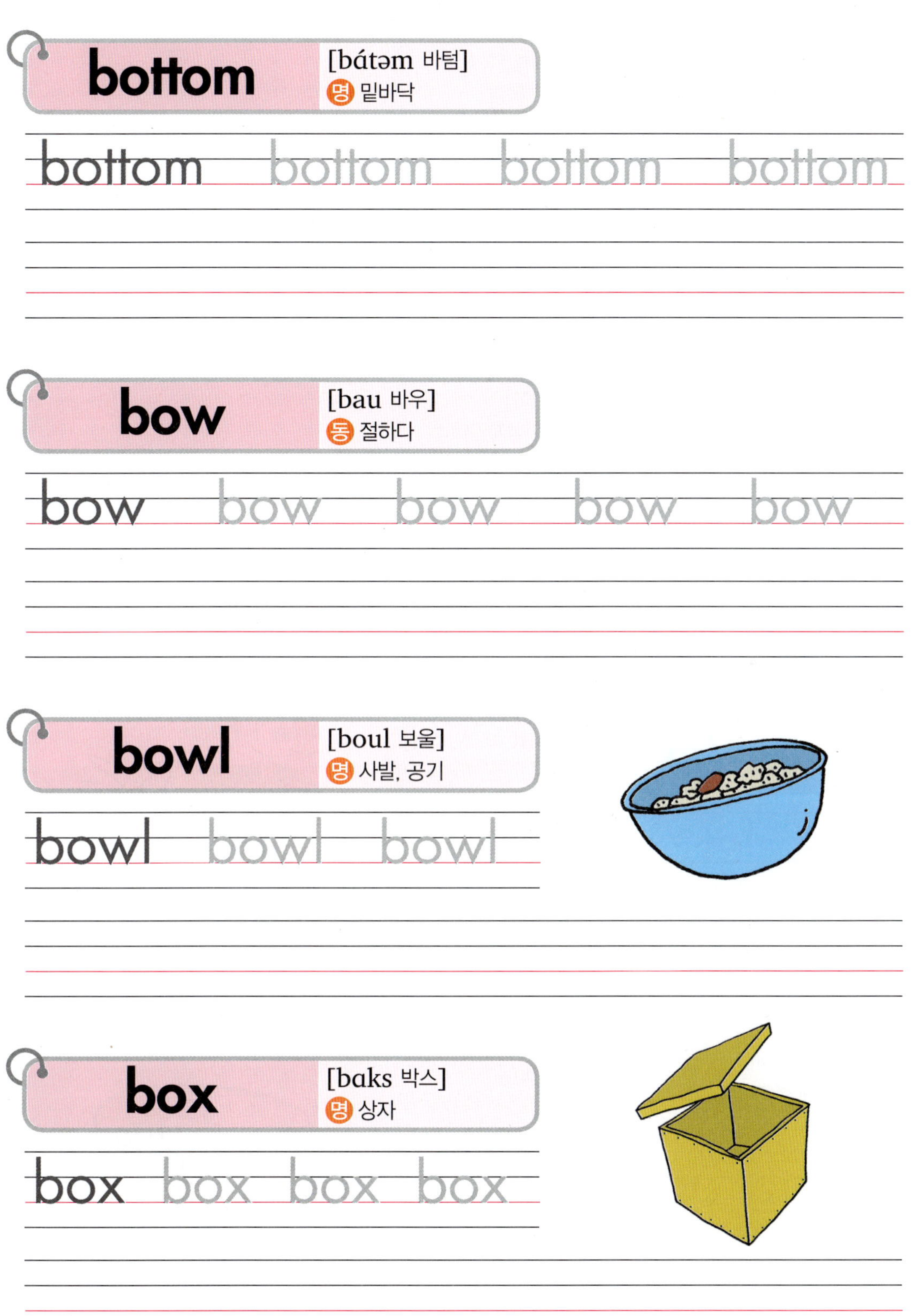

box

[baks 박스]
명 상자

box box box box

boxing

[bǽksiŋ 박싱]
명 권투, 복싱

boxing   boxing   boxing   boxing

boy

[bɔi 보이]
명 소년, 남자 아이

boy boy boy boy boy boy boy

bracelet

[bréislit 브레이스릿]
명 팔찌

bracelet   bracelet

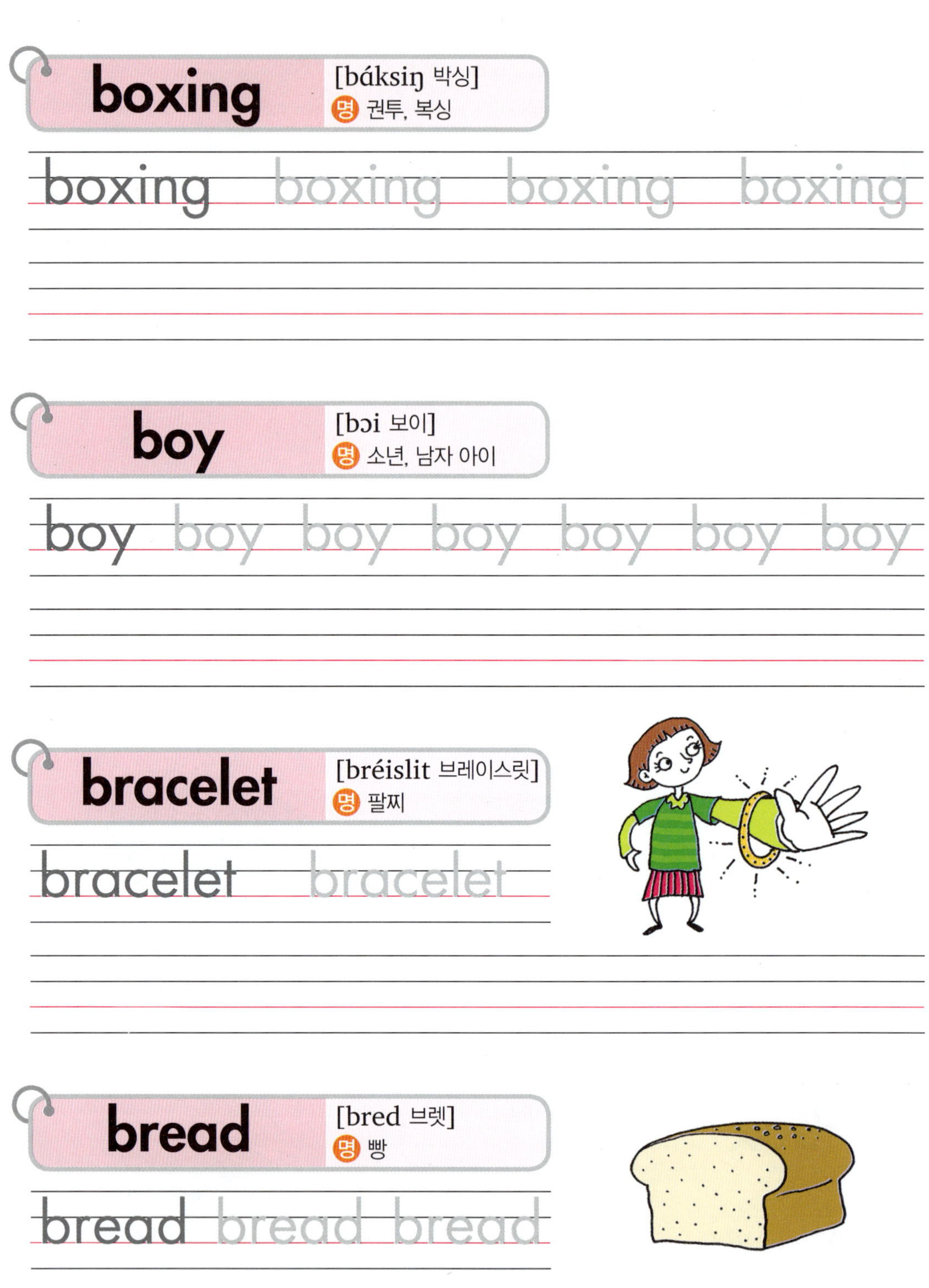

bread

[bred 브렛]
명 빵

bread bread bread

break

[breik 브레이크]
동 깨뜨리다

break break break

breakfast

[brékfəst 브렉퍼스트]
명 아침밥

breakfast breakfast breakfast

bridge

[bridʒ 브리쥐]
명 다리

bridge bridge

bright

[brait 브라이트]
형 빛나는

bright bright bright bright bright

bring

[briŋ 브링]
동 (물건을) 가져오다, (사람을) 데려오다.

bring　bring　bring　bring　bring

Britain

[brít-ən 브리턴]
명 영국

Britain　Britain　Britain　Britain

broom

[bru(:)m 브루(ㅡ)움]
명 비(빗자루)

broom　broom

brother

[brʌðər 브라더]
명 형제

brother　brother

brown
[braun 브라운]
형 갈색의

brown   brown   brown   brown

brush
[brʌʃ 브러쉬]
명 솔

brush   brush   brush

bubble
[bʌ́bəl 버블]
명 거품

bubble   bubble   bubble   bubble

build
[bild 빌드]
동 세우다

build   build   build

building

[bíldiŋ 빌딩]
명 건물

building building building building

bump

[bʌmp 범프]
동 부딪치다.

bump bump bump

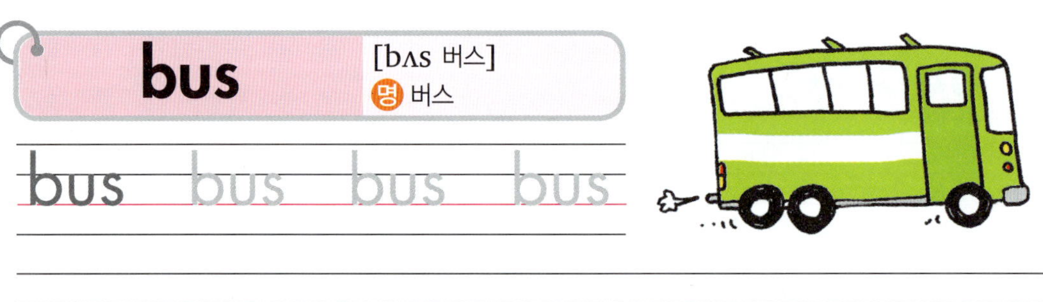

bus

[bʌs 버스]
명 버스

bus bus bus bus

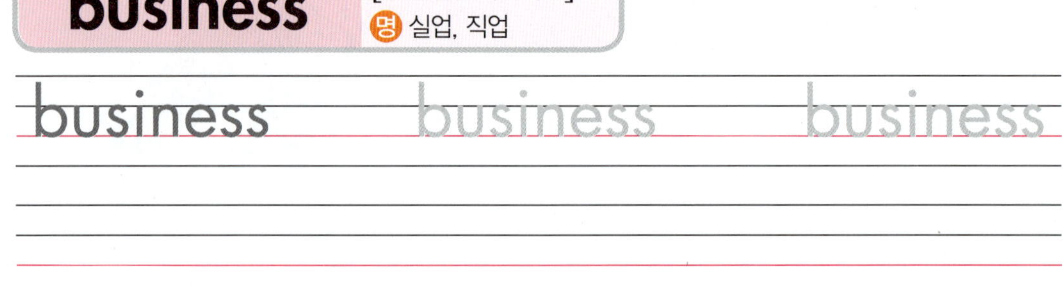

business

[bíznis 비즈니스]
명 실업, 직업

business business business

busy

[bízi 비지]
형 바쁜

busy　busy　busy

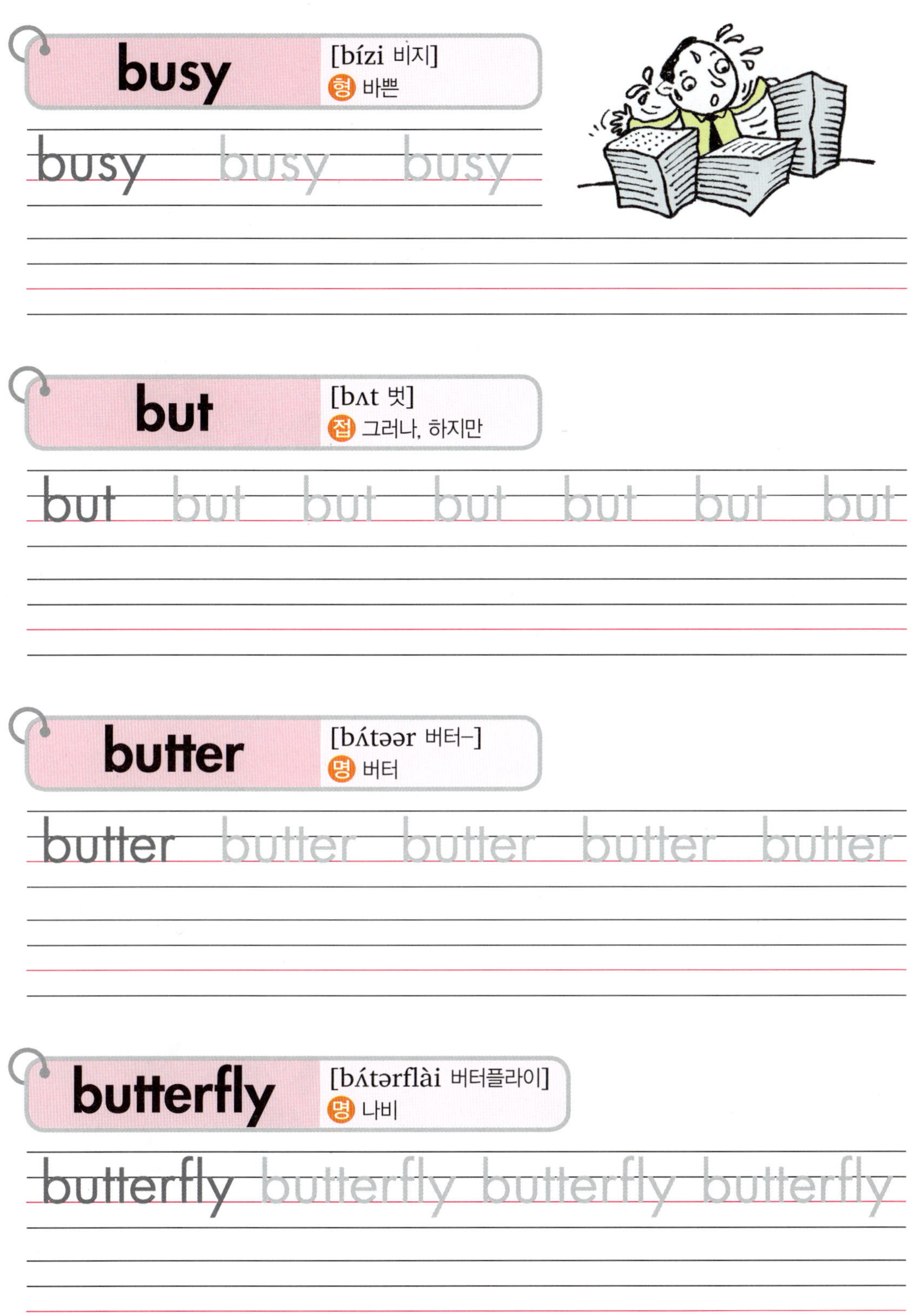

but

[bʌt 벗]
접 그러나, 하지만

but　but　but　but　but　but　but

butter

[bʌ́təər 버터–]
명 버터

butter　butter　butter　butter　butter

butterfly

[bʌ́tərflài 버터플라이]
명 나비

butterfly　butterfly　butterfly　butterfly

button

[bʌ́tn 버튼]
명 단추

button   button   button   button

buy

[bai 바이]
동 사다

buy   buy   buy   buy

by

[bai 바이]
전 ~의 옆에

by   by   by   by   by   by   by   by

bye

[bai 바이]
감 안녕

bye   bye   bye   bye

Cc

cab [kæb 캡]
명 택시

cab　cab　cab　cab　cab　cab

cabbage [kǽbidʒ 캐비쥐]
명 양배추

cabbage　cabbage　cabbage

cage [keidʒ 케이쥐]
명 새장

cage　cage　cage

cake
[keik 케이크]
명 케이크

cake　cake　cake　cake　cake

calendar
[kǽləndər 캘런더]
명 달력

calendar　calendar

call
[kɔːl 코-올]
동 부르다, 전화하다

call　call　call　call　call　call　call

camel
[kǽməl 캐멀]
명 낙타

camel　camel　camel

camera
[kǽmərə 캐머러]
명 카메라

camera   camera

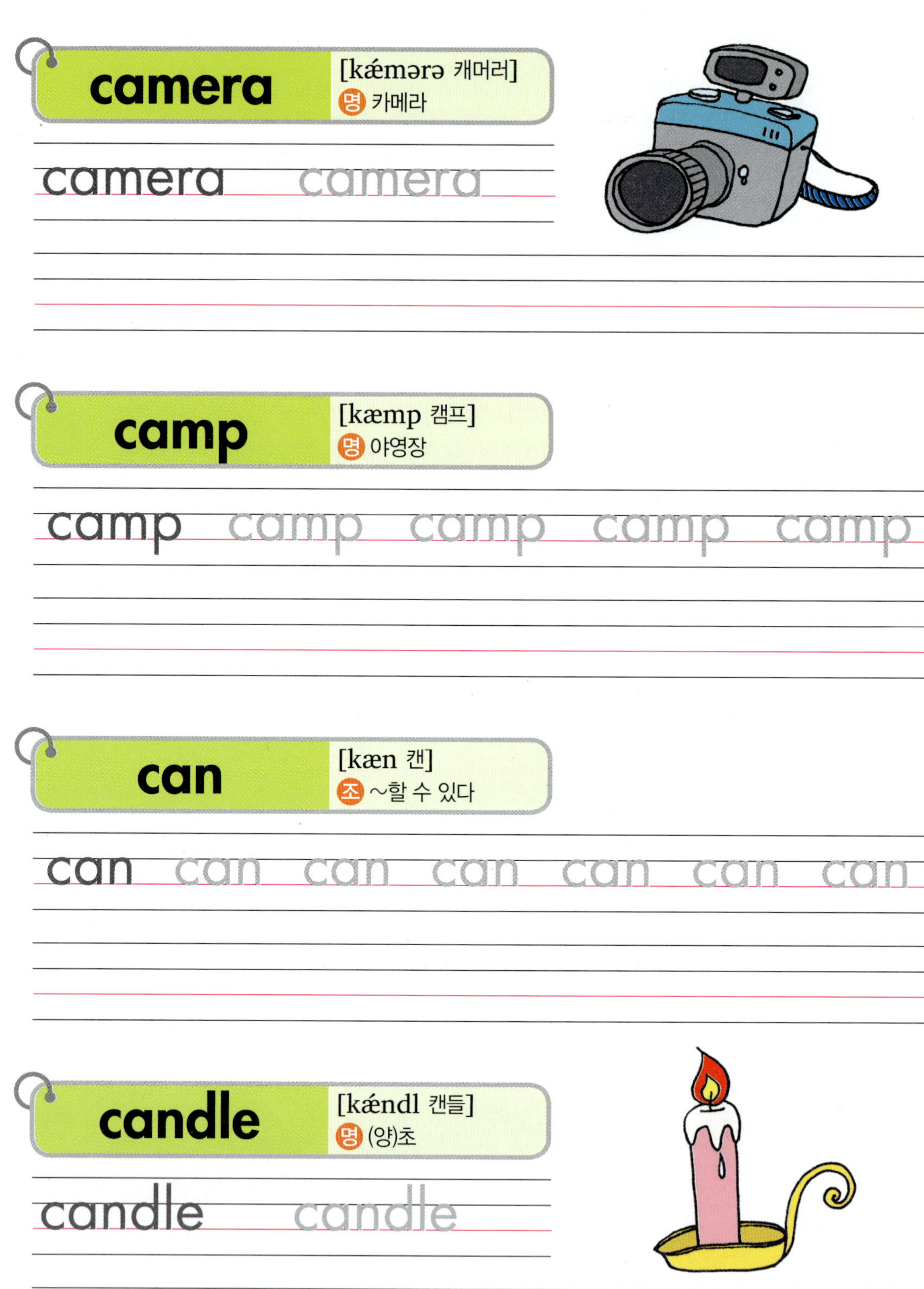

camp
[kæmp 캠프]
명 야영장

camp   camp   camp   camp   camp

can
[kæn 캔]
조 ~할 수 있다

can   can   can   can   can   can   can

candle
[kǽndl 캔들]
명 (양)초

candle   candle

candy

[kǽndi 캔디]
명 사탕

candy   candy   candy   candy

cap

[kæp 캡]
명 모자

cap cap cap cap

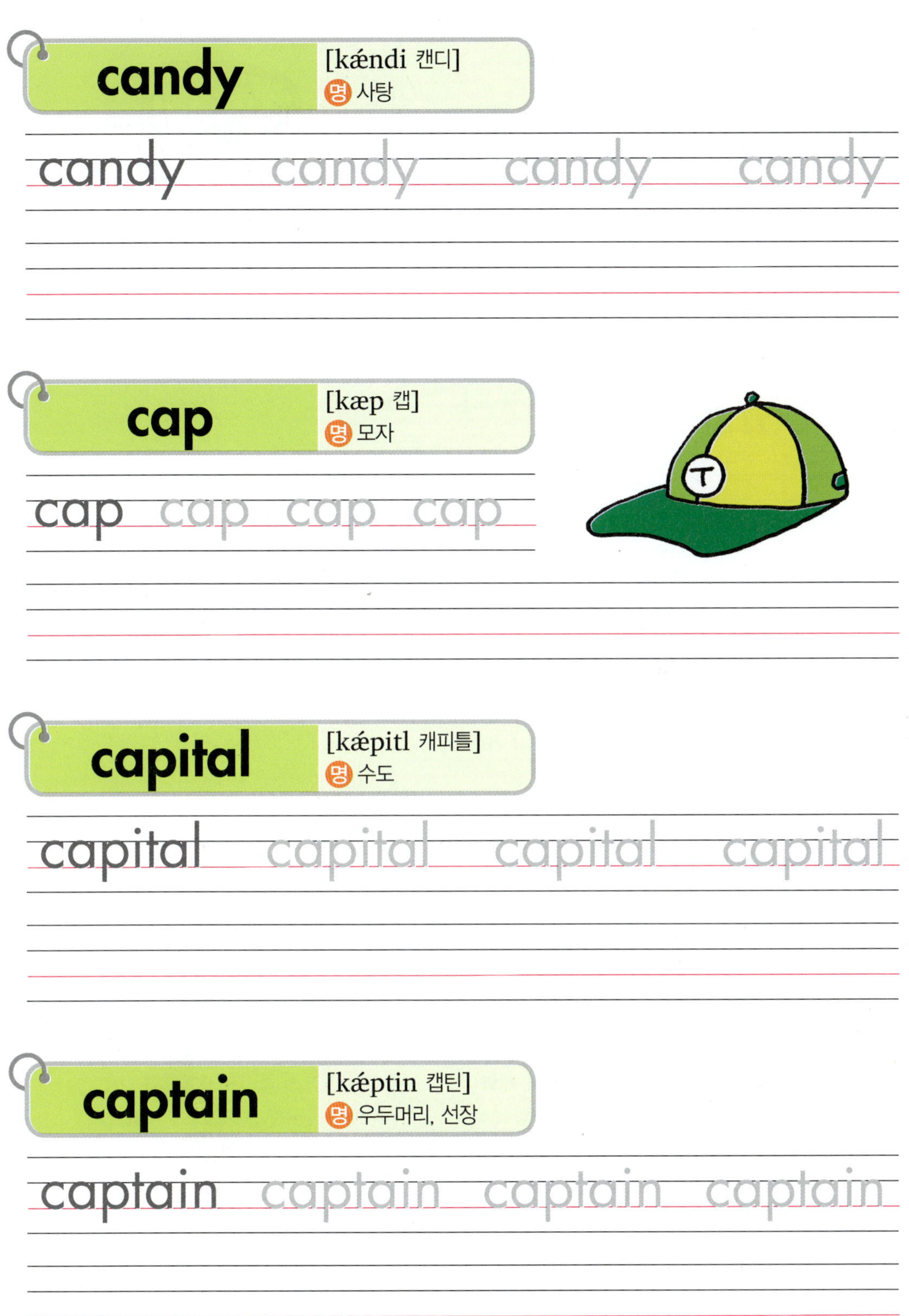

capital

[kǽpitl 캐피틀]
명 수도

capital   capital   capital   capital

captain

[kǽptin 캡틴]
명 우두머리, 선장

captain   captain   captain   captain

car

[kɑːr 카ー]
명 차

car　car　car　car

card

[kɑːrd 카ー드]
명 카드

card　card　card　card　card　card

careful

[kέərfəl 케어펄]
형 주의 깊은

careful　careful　careful　careful

carol

[kǽrəl 캐럴]
명 기쁨의 노래

carol　carol　carol

carpet

[káːrpit 카-핏]
명 카페트, 양탄자

carpet　　carpet　　carpet　　carpet

carrot

[kǽrət 캐럿]
명 당근

carrot　carrot　carrot

carry

[kǽri 캐리]
동 운반하다

carry　carry　carry

cartoon

[kɑːrtúːn 카-투-운]
명 만화

cartoon　cartoon　cartoon　cartoon

cassette

[kæsét 캐셋]
명 카세트

cassette   cassette   cassette   cassette

cat

[kæt 캣]
명 고양이

cat   cat   cat   cat   cat

catch

[kætʃ 캐취]
동 잡다

catch   catch   catch

cave

[keiv 케이브]
명 동굴

cave   cave   cave   cave   cave

ceiling

[síːliŋ 시-일링]
명 천장

ceiling　　ceiling　　ceiling　　ceiling

celebrate

[séləbrèit 셀러브레이트]
동 축하하다

celebrate　　celebrate　　celebrate

center

[séntər 센터]
명 중심, 중앙

center　　center　　center　　center

chair

[tʃɛər 췌어]
명 의자

chair　　chair　　chair

chalk

[tʃɔːk 초-크]
명 분필

chalk   chalk   chalk   chalk   chalk

chance

[tʃæns 챈스]
명 기회

chance   chance   chance   chance

change

[tʃeindʒ 췌인쥐]
동 바꾸다

change   change

cheap

[tʃiːp 취-프]
형 값이 싼

cheap   cheap   cheap   cheap

check
[tʃek 쳌]
동 확인하다

check   check   check

cheese
[tʃiːz 취-즈]
명 치즈

cheese   cheese   cheese   cheese

chicken
[tʃíkin 취킨]
명 닭, 병아리

chicken   chicken

child
[tʃaild 촤일드]
명 아이

child   child   child   child   child

children   children

chin   chin   chin   chin   chin   chin

chocolate   chocolate   chocolate

choice   choice

choose

[tʃuːz 츄-즈]
동 고르다

choose   choose   choose   choose

chopstick

[tʃápstìk 찹스틱]
명 젓가락

chopstick   chopstick

Christmas

[krísməs 크리스마스]
명 크리스마스

Christmas   Christmas   Christmas

church

[tʃəːrtʃ 춰-취]
명 교회

church   church

city

[síti 시티]
명 도시

city   city   city   city

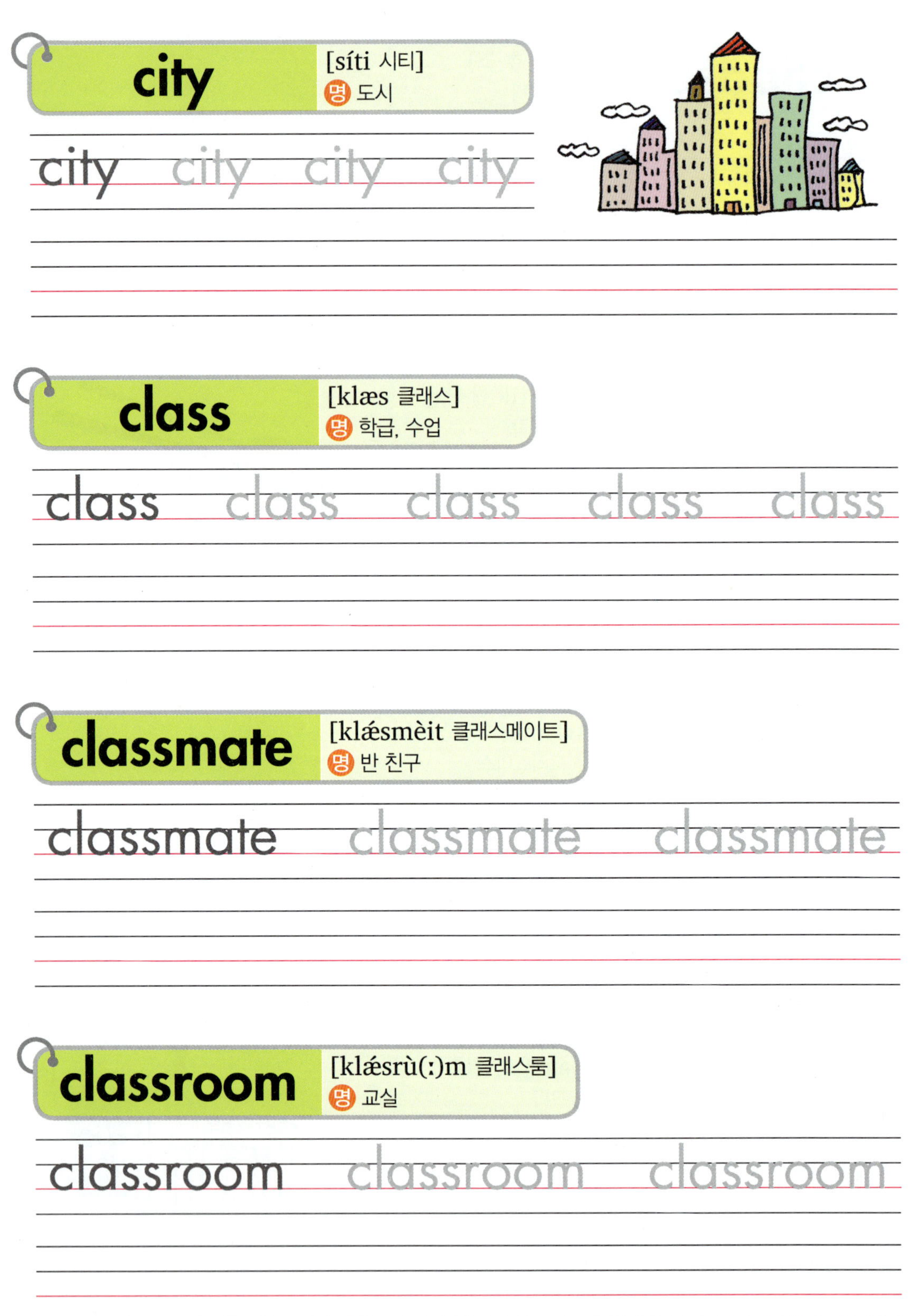

class

[klæs 클래스]
명 학급, 수업

class   class   class   class   class

classmate

[klǽsmèit 클래스메이트]
명 반 친구

classmate   classmate   classmate

classroom

[klǽsrù(:)m 클래스룸]
명 교실

classroom   classroom   classroom

clean

[kliːn 클리-인]
형 깨끗한

clean　clean　clean　clean　clean

clever

[klévər 클레버]
형 영리한

clever　clever　clever　clever　clever

climb

[klaim 클라임]
동 오르다

climb　climb　climb

clock

[klɑk 클락]
명 시계

clock　clock　clock

close

[klouz 클로우즈]
동 닫다, (눈을)감다

close　close　close

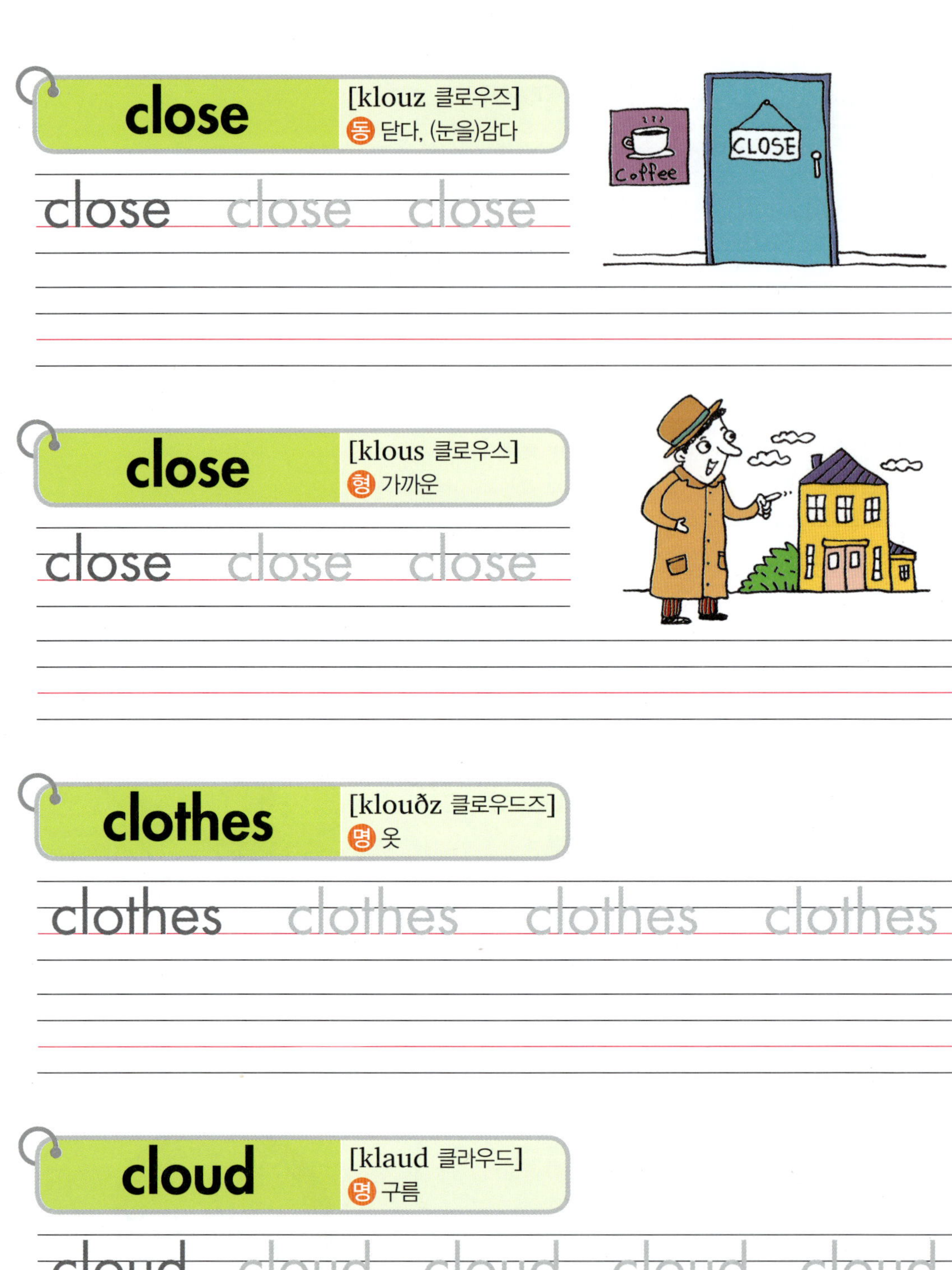

close

[klous 클로우스]
형 가까운

close　close　close

clothes

[klouðz 클로우드즈]
명 옷

clothes　clothes　clothes　clothes

cloud

[klaud 클라우드]
명 구름

cloud　cloud　cloud　cloud　cloud

cloudy

[kláudi 클라우디]
형 흐린, 구름이 많은

cloudy　cloudy　cloudy　cloudy

club

[klʌb 클럽]
명 클럽, 동호회

club　club　club　club　club　club

coast

[koust 코우스트]
명 바닷가

coast　coast　coast　coast　coast

coat

[kout 코우트]
명 외투, 코트

coat coat coat coat

coffee

[kɔ́:fi 코-피]
명 커피

coffee coffee coffee

coin

[kɔin 코인]
명 동전, 돈

coin coin coin coin coin coin

cold

[kould 코울드]
형 추운, 찬

cold cold cold cold

college

[kálidʒ 칼리쥐]
명 대학

college college college college

58

color

[kʌ́lər 컬러]
명 색, 빛깔

color　color　color　color　color

come

[kʌm 컴]
동 오다

come　come　come

comedy

[kámədi 카머디]
명 희극, 코미디

comedy　comedy　comedy　comedy

computer

[kəmpjúːtər 컴퓨–터]
명 컴퓨터

computer　computer

continue

[kəntínju: 컨티뉴-]
동 계속되다.

continue   continue   continue

cook

[kuk 쿡]
동 요리하다

cook   cook   cook

cool

[ku:l 쿠-울]
형 서늘(시원)한

cool   cool   cool   cool   cool   cool

copy

[kápi 카피]
명 복사

copy   copy   copy   copy   copy

correct

[kərékt 커렉트]
형 옳은, 정확한

correct   correct

corn

[kɔːrn 코-온]
명 옥수수

corn corn corn corn

corner

[kɔ́ːrnər 코-너]
명 모퉁이

corner   corner   corner   corner

cotton

[kátn 카튼]
명 솜, 면화

cotton   cotton   cotton   cotton

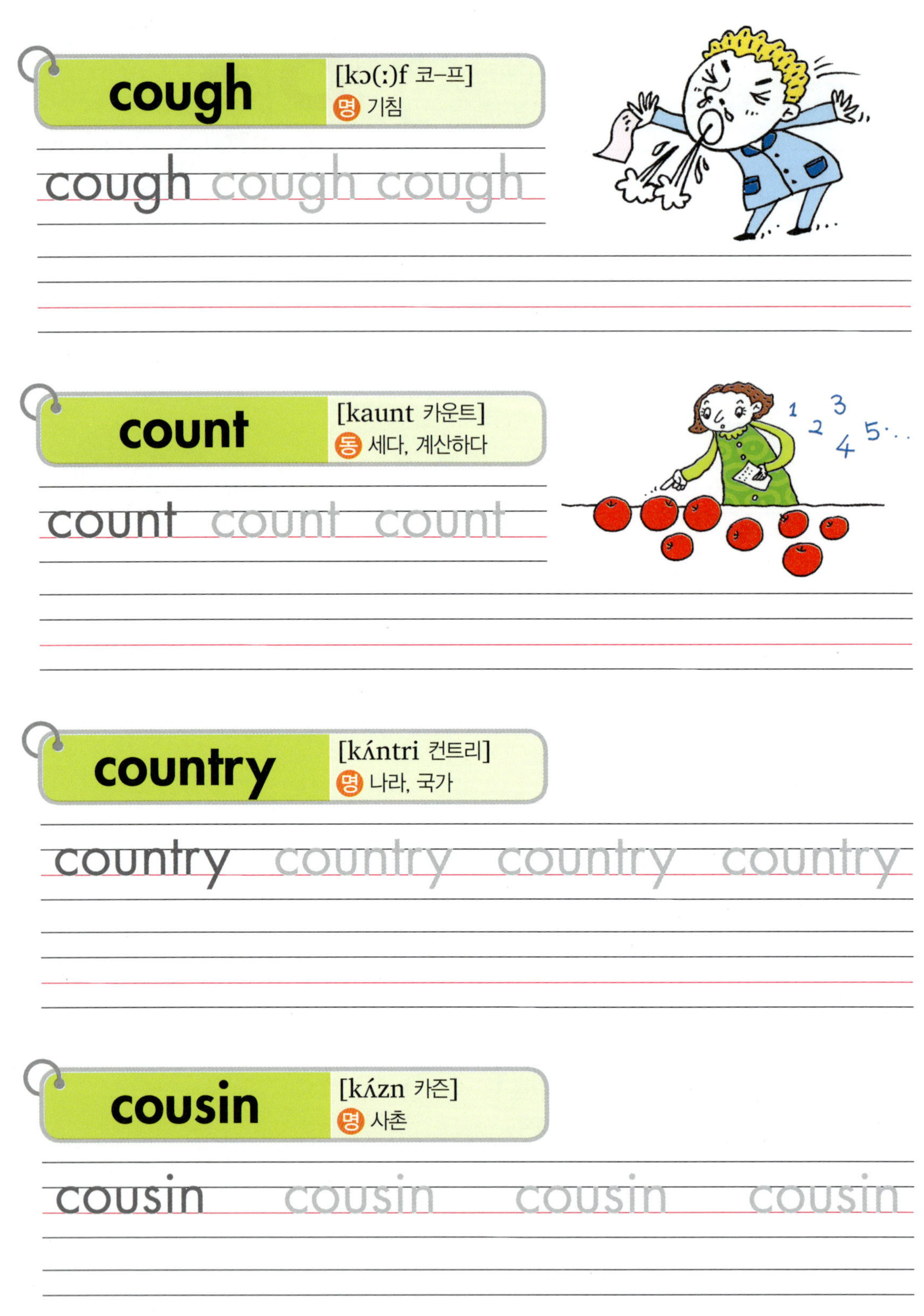

cough

[kɔ(ː)f 코-프]
명 기침

cough cough cough

count

[kaunt 카운트]
동 세다, 계산하다

count count count

country

[kʌ́ntri 컨트리]
명 나라, 국가

country country country country

cousin

[kʌ́zn 카즌]
명 사촌

cousin cousin cousin cousin

cover

[kʌ́vər 커버]
동 덮다.

cover cover cover

cow

[kau 카우]
명 암소

cow cow cow cow cow cow

crab

[kræb 크랩]
명 게

crab crab crab crab

crayon

[kréiən 크레이언]
명 크레용

crayon crayon crayon crayon

cream

[kri:m 크리-임]
명 크림

cream cream cream cream

cross

[krɔːs 크로-스]
동 건너다

cross cross cross cross cross cross

crown

[kraun 크라운]
명 왕관, 왕위

crown crown crown

cry

[krai 크라이]
동 울다, 외치다

cry cry cry cry

culture

[kʌ́ltʃər 컬춰]
명 문화

culture   culture   culture   culture

cup

[kʌp 컵]
명 찻잔, 컵

cup   cup   cup   cup   cup   cup   cup

curious

[kjúəriəs 큐어리어스]
형 호기심이 많은

curious   curious

curtain

[kə́ːrtən 커-턴]
명 커텐

curtain   curtain

cut

[kʌt 컷]
동 베다, 자르다

cut   cut   cut   cut   cut

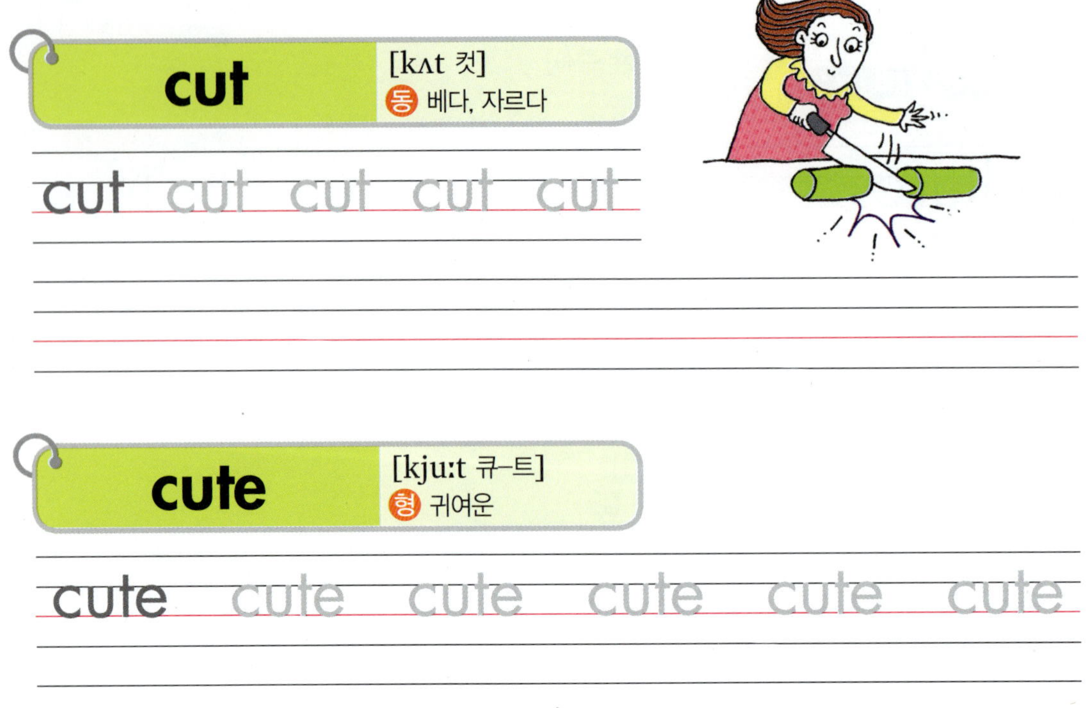

cute

[kju:t 큐―트]
형 귀여운

cute   cute   cute   cute   cute

A
B
G
W

Dd

dad

[dæd 댓]
명 아빠

dad   dad   dad   dad   dad   dad

daily

[déili 데일리]
형 매일의

daily   daily   daily   daily   daily

dance

[dæns 댄스]
동 춤추다

dance dance dance

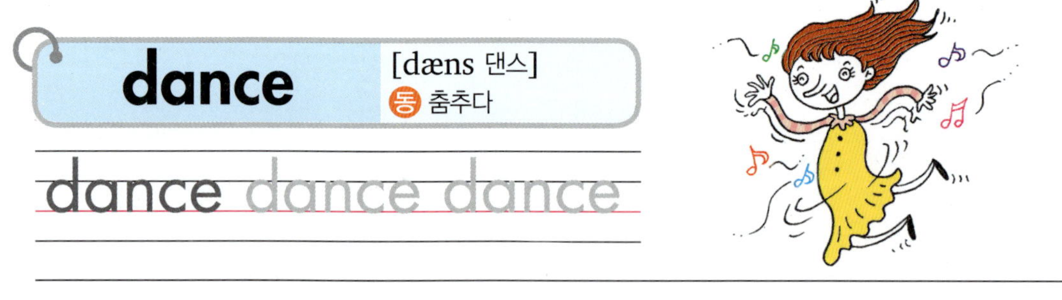

dancing

[dǽnsiŋ 댄싱]
명 춤

dancing dancing dancing dancing

dancer

[dǽnsər 댄서]
명 춤추는 사람

dancer dancer dancer dancer

danger

[déindʒər 데인줘]
명 위험

danger danger

dark

[dɑːrk 다-크]
형 어두운

dark dark dark dark dark dark

date

[deit 데이트]
명 날짜

date　date　date　date　date　date

daughter

[dɔ́:tər 도-터]
명 딸

daughter　daughter

day

[dei 데이]
명 낮, 하루, 날

day　day　day　day　day　day

dead

[ded 뎃]
형 죽은

dead　dead　dead

deaf

[def 데프]
형 귀머거리의

deaf　deaf　deaf　deaf　deaf　deaf

dear

[diər 디어]
형 사랑하는

dear　dear　dear

death

[deθ 데쓰]
명 죽음

death　death　death　death　death

December

[disémbər 디셈버]
명 12월

December　December　December

deep

[di:p 디-입]
형 깊은

deep　deep　deep

deer

[diər 디어]
명 사슴

deer　deer　deer　deer　deer　deer

delicious

[dilíʃəs 딜리셔스]
형 맛있는

delicious　delicious

dentist

[déntist 덴티스트]
명 치과의사

dentist　dentist　dentist　dentist

department store [dipá:rtmənt stɔ:r 디파-트먼트스토-]
명 백화점

department store　department store

desk [desk 데스크]
명 책상

desk　desk　desk

dial [dáiəl 다이얼]
동 전화 걸다.

dial　dial　dial　dial

diary [dáiəri 다이어리]
명 일기, 일기장

diary　diary　diary　diary　diary

dictionary [díkʃənèri 딕셔네리]
명 사전

dictionary dictionary

die [dai 다이]
동 죽다

die die die die die die die

difference [dífərəns 디퍼런스]
명 다름, 차이

difference difference difference

different [dífərənt 디퍼런트]
형 다른

different different

difficult

[dífikʌ̀lt 디피컬트]
형 어려운

difficult　difficult　difficult　difficult

dinner

[dínər 디너]
명 저녁식사

dinner　dinner　dinner　dinner

dinosaur

[dáinəsɔ̀:r 다이너소―]
명 공룡

dinosaur　dinosaur

dirty

[dɔ́:rti 더―티]
형 더러운

dirty dirty dirty dirty

discount

discount discount discount discount

dish

dish dish dish dish dish dish

doctor

doctor doctor doctor doctor

dog

dog dog dog dog

doll

[dɑl 달]
명 인형

doll　doll　doll　doll

dollar

[dálər 달러]
명 달러(미국의 돈)

dollar　dollar　dollar　dollar　dollar

dolphin

[dálfin 달핀]
명 돌고래

dolphin　dolphin

donkey

[dáŋki 당키]
명 당나귀

donkey　donkey　donkey　donkey

door

[dɔːr 도-]
명 문, 방문

door　door　door

double

[dʌbəl 더블]
형 두 배의

double　double　double　double

down

[daun 다운]
부 아래에

down　down　down

downstairs

[daunstέərz 다운스테어즈]
부 아래층에

downstairs　downstairs　downstairs

dragon
[drǽgən 드래건]
명 용

dragon　dragon　dragon　dragon

draw¹
[drɔː 드로―]
동 끌다, 당기다

draw　draw　draw

draw²
[drɔː 드로―]
동 (그림을)그리다

draw　draw　draw

dream
[driːm 드리―임]
명 꿈

dream　dream　dream　dream

dress

[dres 드레스]
동 옷을 입히다

dress   dress   dress   dress   dress

drink

[driŋk 드링크]
동 마시다

drink   drink   drink

drive

[draiv 드라이브]
동 운전하다

drive   drive   drive   drive   drive

drop

[drɑp 드랍]
동 떨어뜨리다

drop   drop   drop

drum

[drʌm 드럼]
명 북

drum　drum　drum

dry

[drai 드라이]
형 마른, 건조한

dry　dry　dry　dry

duck

[dʌk 덕]
명 오리

duck　duck　duck　duck　duck

during

[djúəriŋ 듀어링]
전 ～동안, ～사이에

during　during　during　during

dust

[dʌst 더스트]
명 먼지

dust dust dust dust

G
S
A
M

Ee

each

[[iːtʃ 이-취]
형 각각의

each　each　each　each　each

eagle

[íːgəl 이-걸]
명 독수리

eagle　eagle　eagle　eagle　eagle

ear

[[iər 이어]
명 귀

ear　ear　ear　ear

early

[ə́:rli 어-얼리]
부 일찍이, 일찍

early　early　early　early　early

earth

[ə:rɵ 어-쓰]
명 지구

earth　earth　earth　earth　earth

east

[i:st 이-스트]
명 동쪽

east　east　east　east

easy

[í:zi 이-지]
형 쉬운

easy　easy　easy　easy　easy　easy

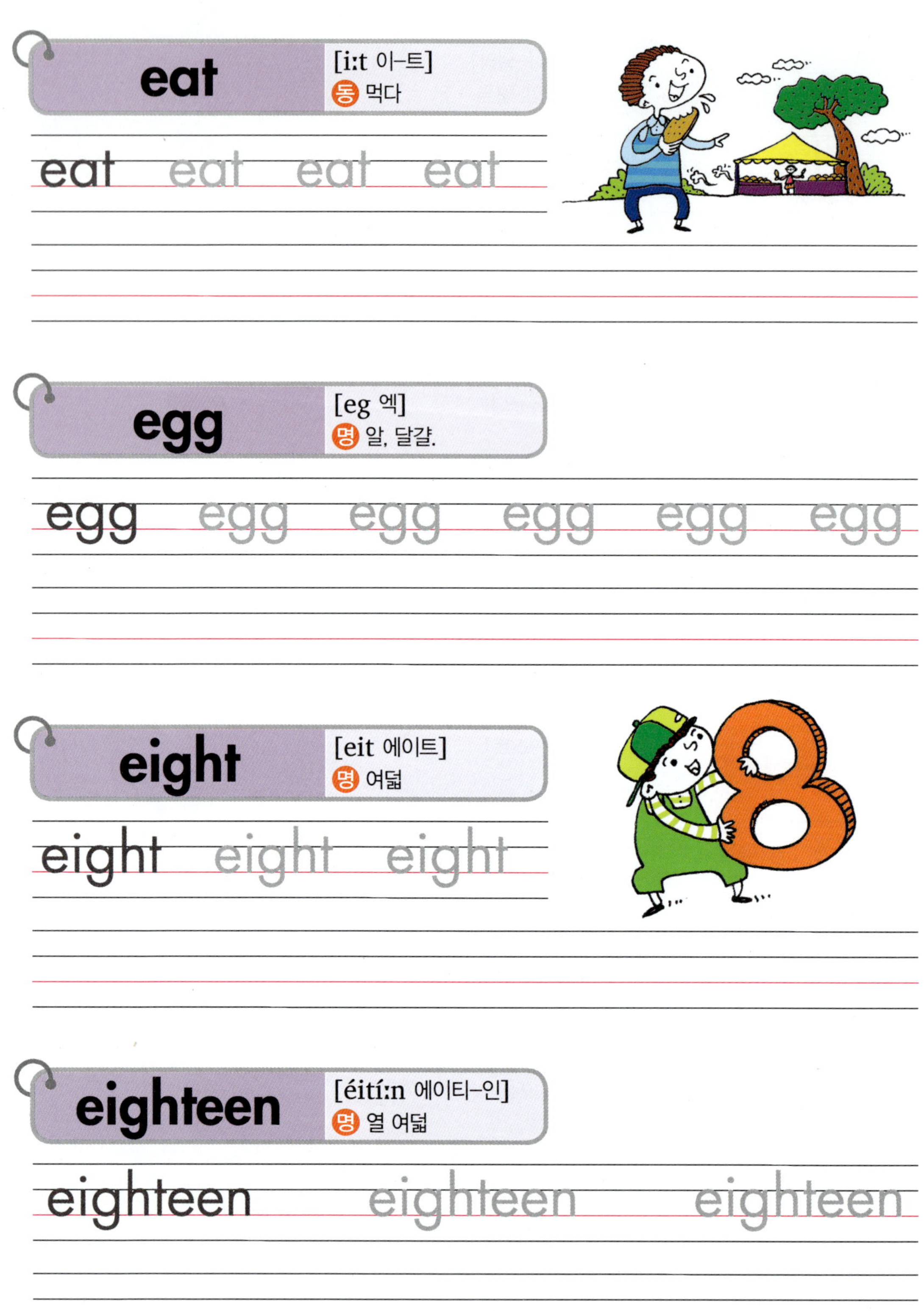

eat

[i:t 이-트]
동 먹다

eat   eat   eat   eat

egg

[eg 엑]
명 알, 달걀.

egg   egg   egg   egg   egg   egg

eight

[eit 에이트]
명 여덟

eight   eight   eight

eighteen

[éití:n 에이티-인]
명 열 여덟

eighteen   eighteen   eighteen

eighty

[éiti 에이티]
명 80, 여든

eighty eighty eighty

elbow

[élbou 엘보우]
명 팔꿈치

elbow elbow elbow elbow

elephant

[éləfənt 엘러펀트]
명 코끼리

elephant elephant

elevator

[éləvèitər 엘러베이터]
명 엘리베이터

elevator elevator elevator elevator

eleven

[ilévən 일레번]
명 열 하나

eleven　　eleven　　eleven　　eleven

empty

[émpti 엠프티]
형 비어있는

empty empty empty

end

[end 엔드]
명 끝

end　end　end　end　end　end　end

energy

[énərdʒi 에너쥐]
명 에너지, 힘

energy　　energy

enjoy

[endʒɔ́i 엔죠이]
동 즐기다

enjoy enjoy enjoy enjoy enjoy

enough

[inʌ́f 이너프]
형 충분한

enough enough enough enough

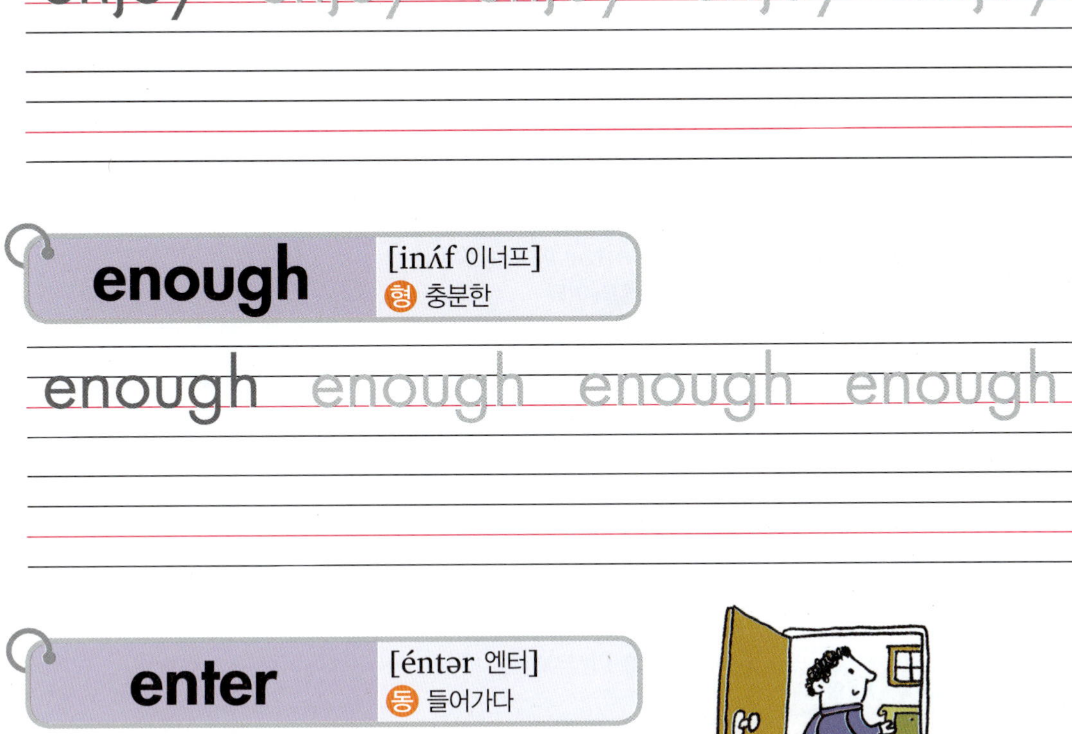

enter

[éntər 엔터]
동 들어가다

enter enter enter

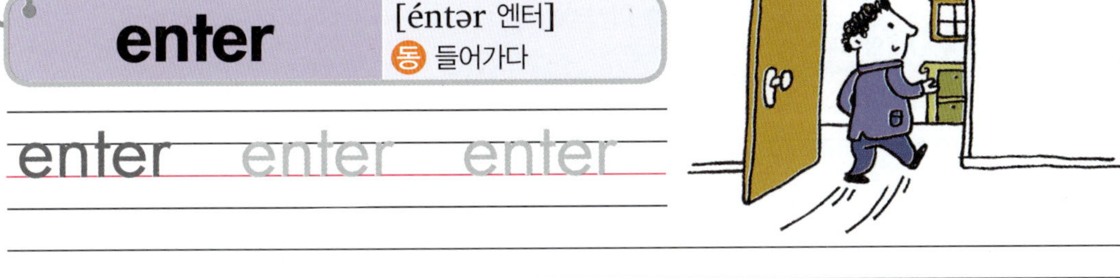

equal

[íːkwəl 이-퀄]
형 같은

equal equal equal

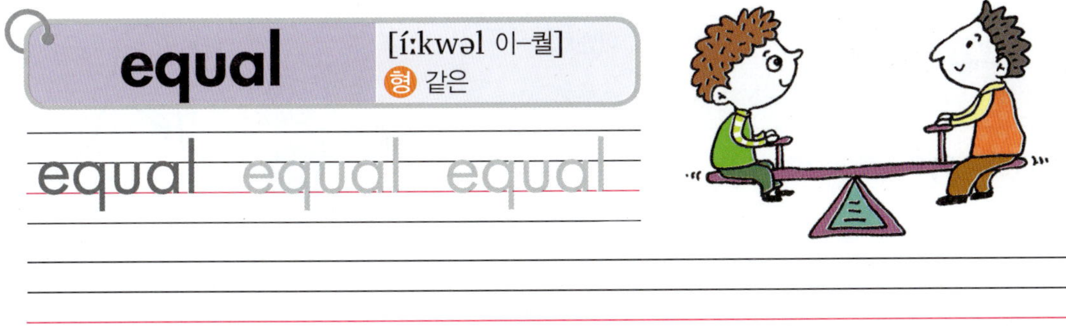

eraser

[iréisər 이레이서]
명 지우는 사람, 지우개

eraser   eraser   eraser   eraser

escalator

[éskəlèitər 에스컬레이터]
명 에스컬레이터

escalator   escalator   escalator

evening

[íːvniŋ 이-브닝]
명 저녁

evening evening evening evening

event

[ivént 이벤트]
명 사건

event event event

every

[évri: 에브리-]
형 모든

every　every　every

example

[igzǽmpəl 이그잼펄]
명 예, 보기

example　example　example

excited

[iksáitid 익사이팃]
형 흥분한

excited　excited

exciting

[iksáitiŋ 익사이팅]
형 흥분시키는

exciting　exciting　exciting　exciting

excuse

[ikskjú:z 익스큐–즈]
동 용서하다

excuse   excuse   excuse   excuse

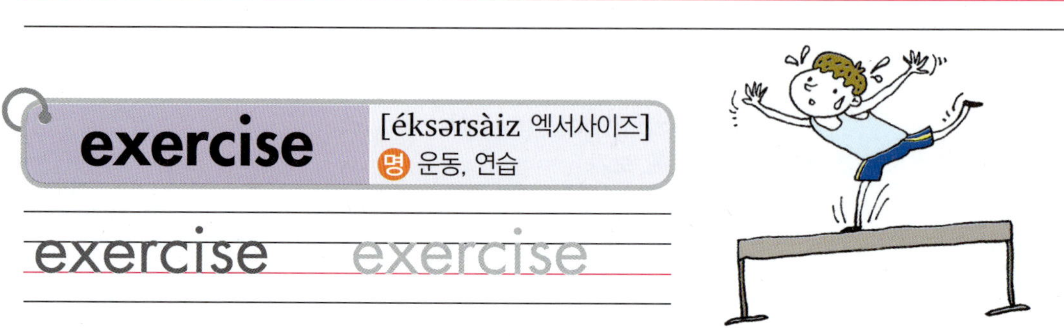

exercise

[éksərsàiz 엑서사이즈]
명 운동, 연습

exercise   exercise

exit

[éksit 엑싯]
명 출구

exit   exit   exit   exit

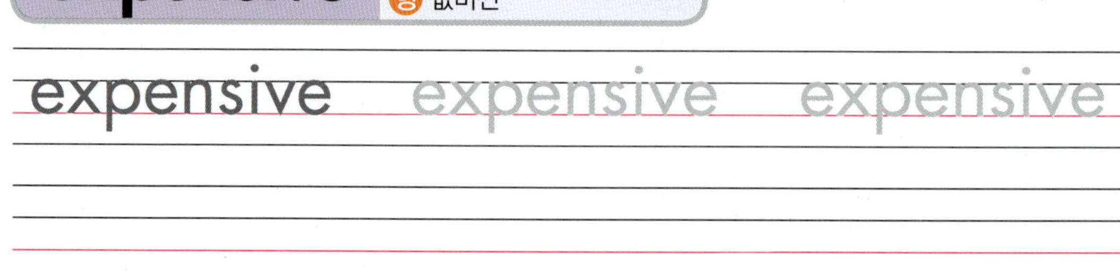

expensive

[ikspénsiv 익스펜시브]
형 값비싼

expensive   expensive   expensive

explain

[ikspléin 익스플레인]
동 설명하다

explain   explain

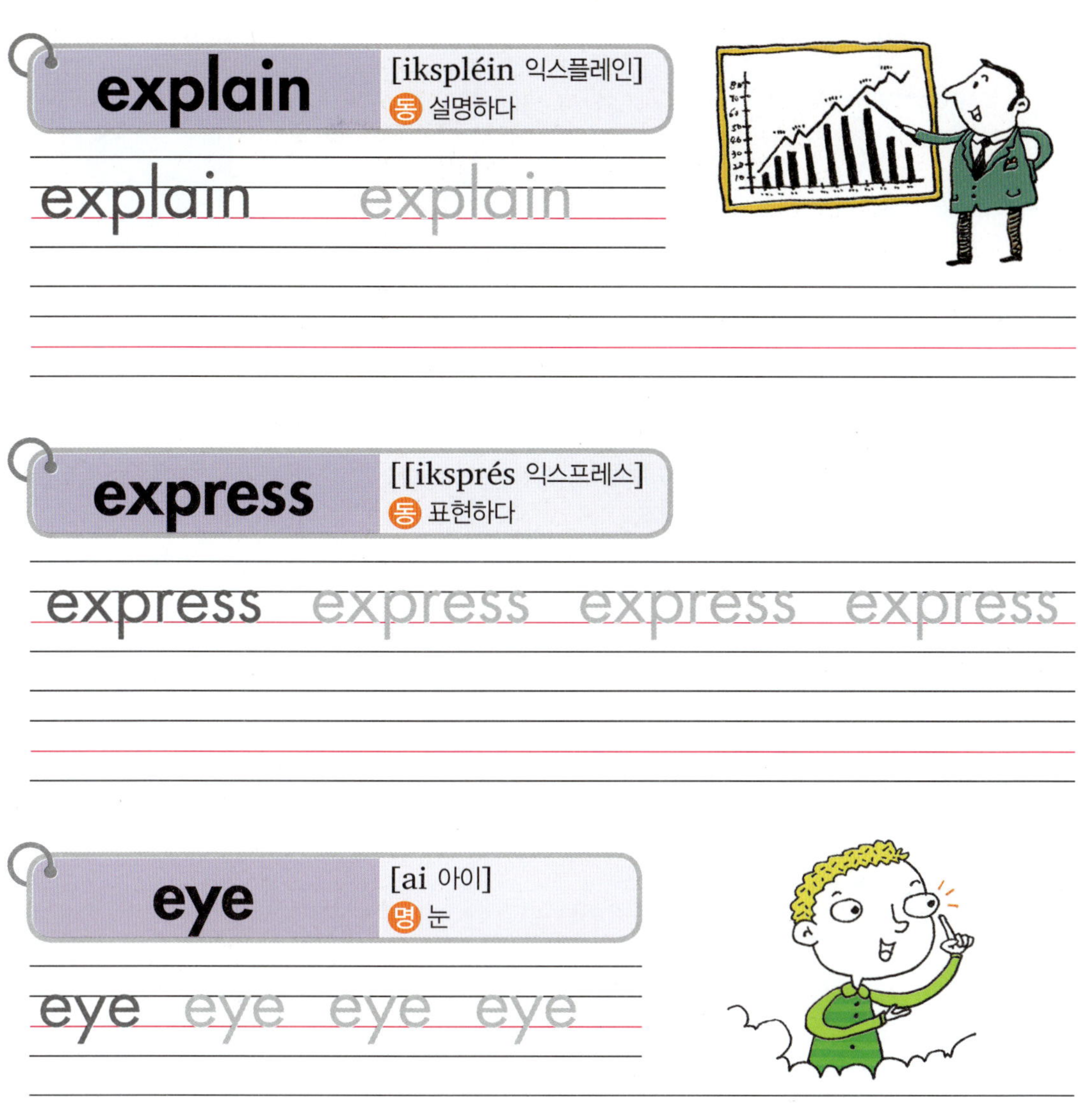

express

[[iksprés 익스프레스]
동 표현하다

express   express   express   express

eye

[ai 아이]
명 눈

eye   eye   eye   eye

Ff

face
[feis 페이스]
명 얼굴

face face face face face face

fact
[fækt 팩트]
명 사실

fact fact fact fact fact fact fact

fail
[feil 페일]
동 실패하다

fail fail fail fail

fair

[fɛər 페어]
형 공평한, 올바른

fair fair fair fair fair fair fair

fall¹

[fɔːl 포―올]
명 가을

fall fall fall fall

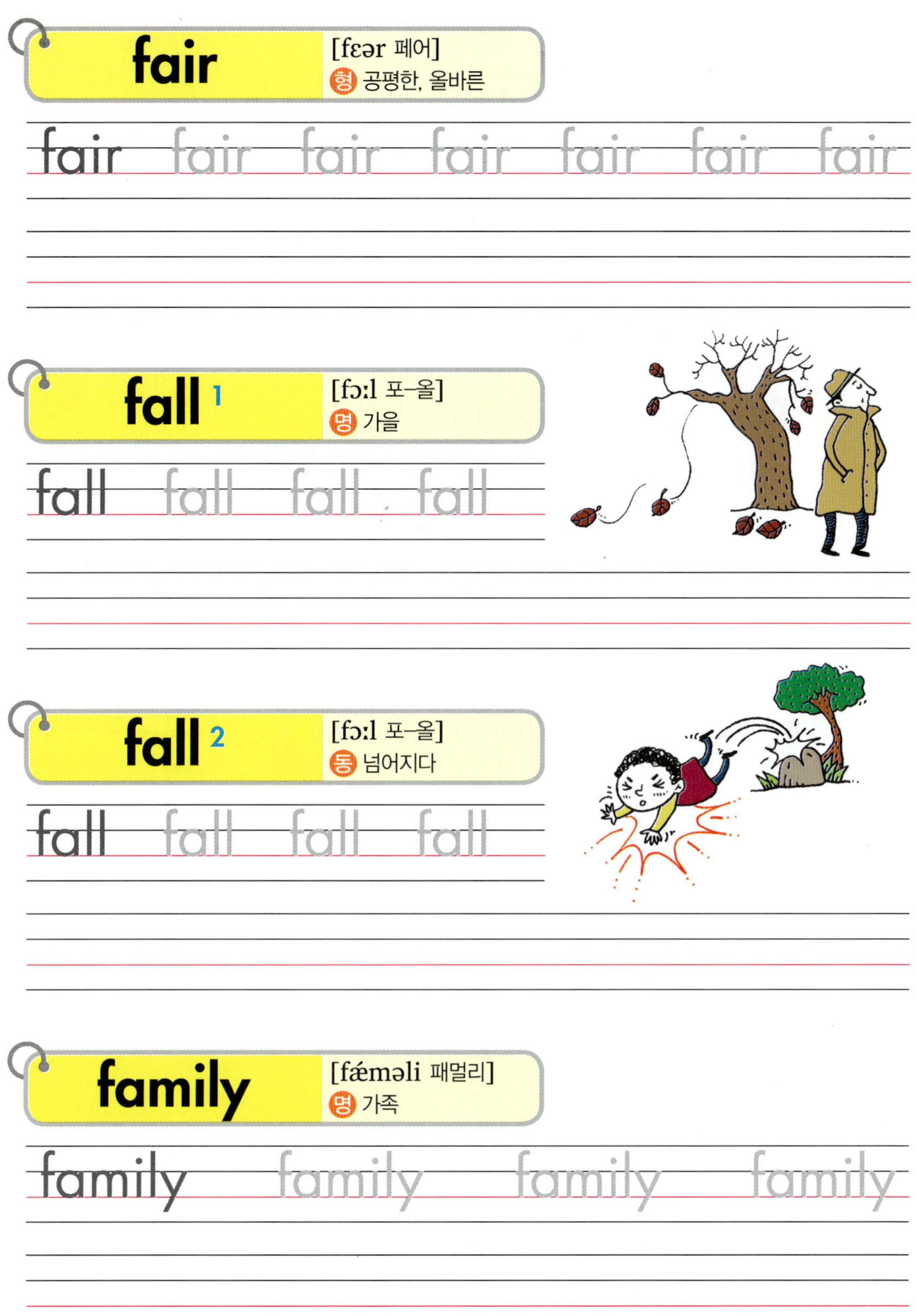

fall²

[fɔːl 포―올]
동 넘어지다

fall fall fall fall

family

[fǽməli 패멀리]
명 가족

family family family family

famous

[féiməs 페이머스]
형 유명한

famous   famous   famous   famous

fan

[fæn 팬]
명 부채, 선풍기

fan   fan   fan   fan   fan   fan   fan

far

[fɑːr 파–]
부 멀리

far   far   far   far   far

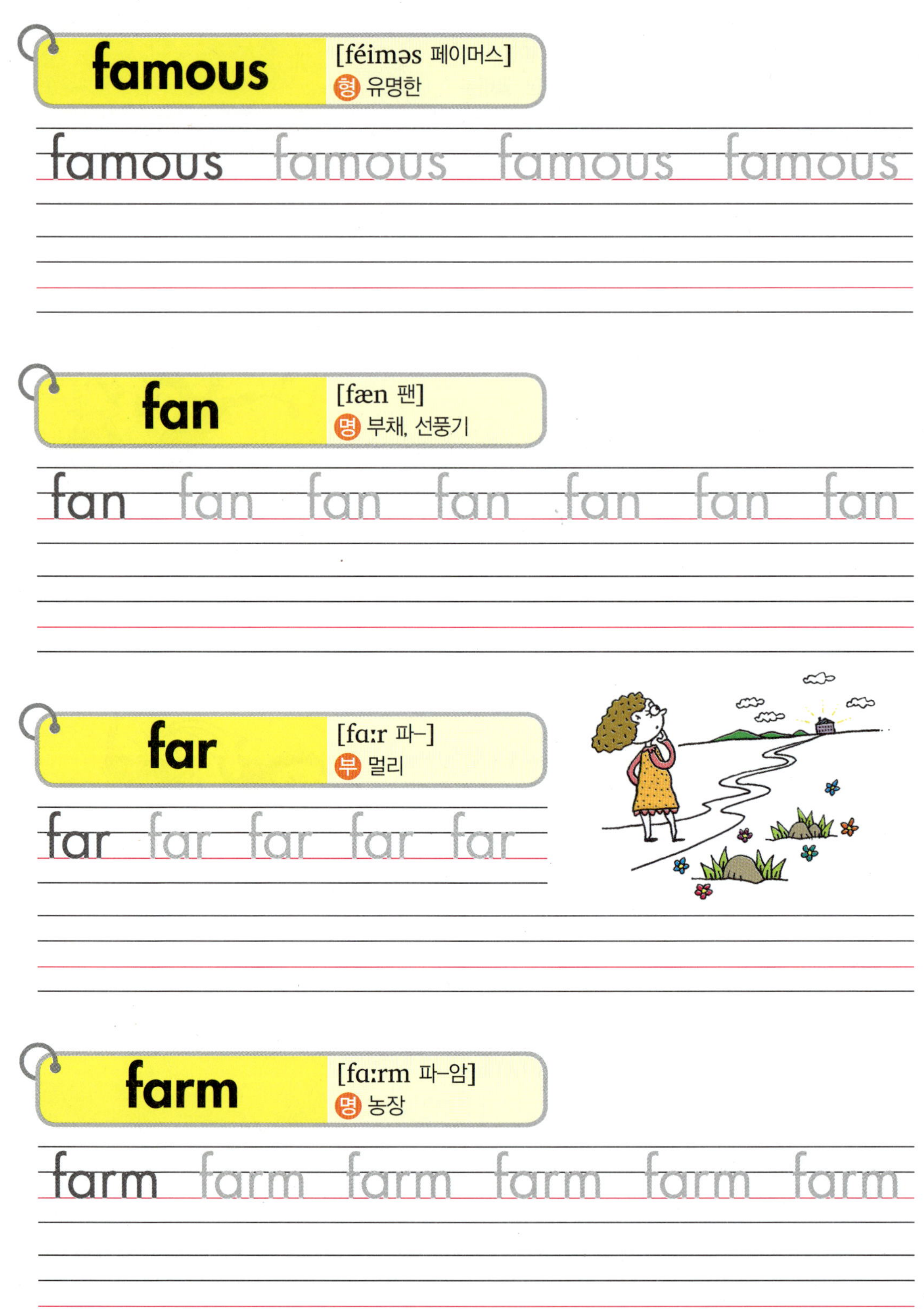

farm

[fɑːrm 파–암]
명 농장

farm   farm   farm   farm   farm   farm

farmer

farmer [fá:rmər 파-머] 명 농부

farmer　farmer

fast

fast [fæst 패스트] 형 빠른

fast fast fast fast fast fast fast

fat

fat [fæt 팻] 형 살찐

fat fat fat fat fat

father

father [fá:ðər 파-더] 명 아버지

father father father father father

favorite

[féivərit 페이버릿]
형 마음에 드는

favorite　favorite

February

[fébruèri 페브루에리]
명 2월

February　February　February

feel

[fi:l 피-일]
동 느끼다

feel feel feel feel

feeling

[fíːliŋ 피-일링]
명 감각, 느낌

feeling feeling feeling feeling

fellow

[félou 펠로우]
명 동무, 친구

fellow fellow fellow

field

[fi:ld 피-일드]
명 들(판)

field field field field field field

fifteen

[fìftí:n 피프티-인]
명 열 다섯

fifteen fifteen fifteen

fifty

[fífti 피프티]
명 50, 쉰

fifty fifty fifty fifty fifty fifty fifty

fight
[fait 파이트]
동 싸우다

fight   fight   fight   fight   fight   fight

fill
[fil 필]
동 채우다

fill   fill   fill   fill   fill

film
[film 필름]
명 영화

film   film   film   film   film   film   film

find
[faind 파인드]
동 발견하다

find   find   find   find

fine

[fain 파인]
형 좋은, 훌륭한

fine　fine　fine　fine　fine　fine　fine

finger

[fíŋgər 핑거]
명 손가락

finger　finger　finger　finger　finger

finish

[fíniʃ 피니쉬]
동 끝내다

finish　finish　finish　finish　finish

fire

[faiər 파이어]
명 불

fire　fire　fire　fire

fireman

[faiə́rmən 파이어먼]
명 소방관

fireman fireman fireman fireman

first

[fə:rst 퍼—스트]
형 첫번째의

first first first first first first first

fish

[fiʃ 피쉬]
명 물고기

fish fish fish fish

five

[faiv 파이브]
명 다섯

five five five five five five five

flag

[flæg 플래그]
명 기(깃발)

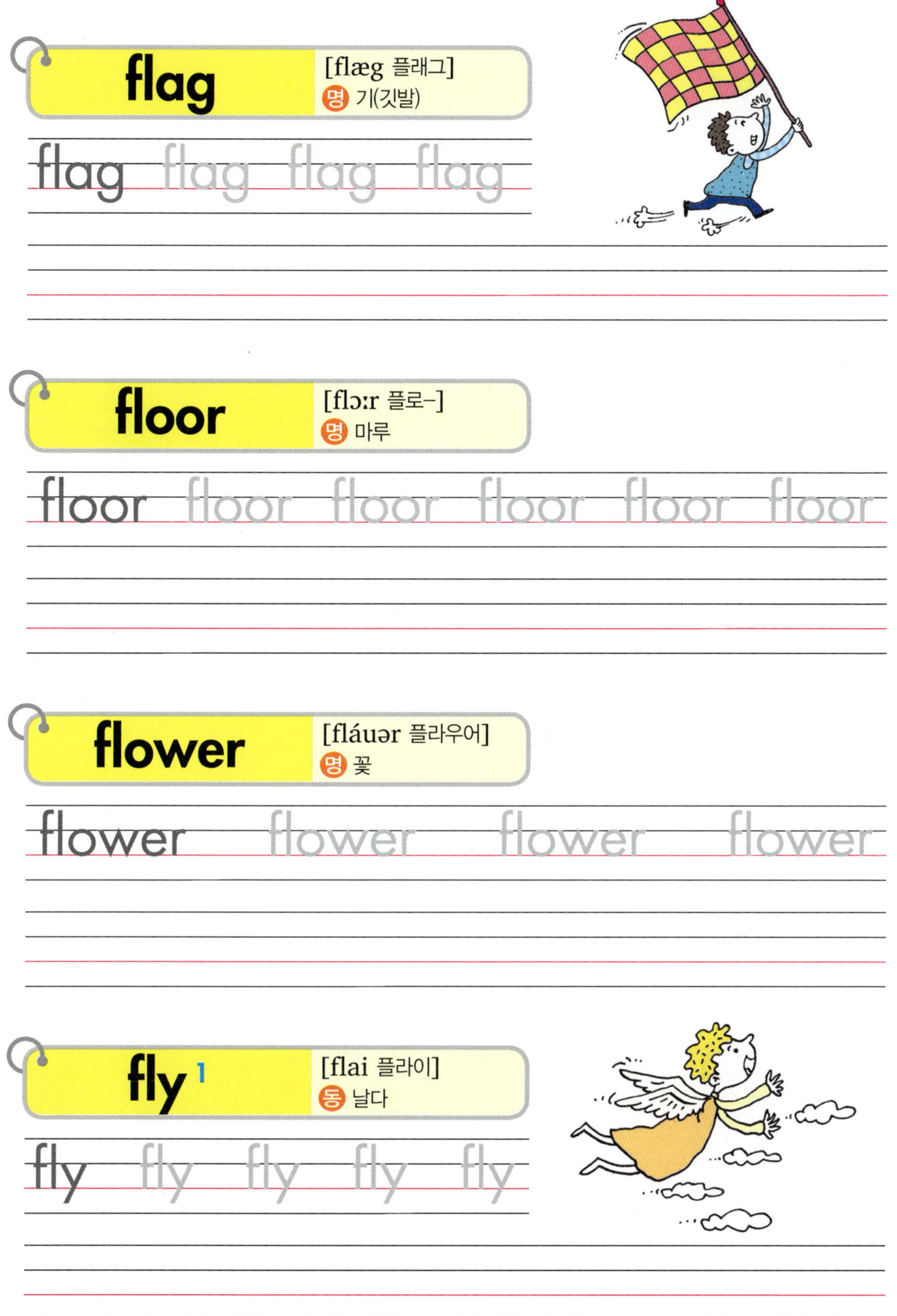

flag　flag　flag　flag

floor

[flɔ:r 플로–]
명 마루

floor　floor　floor　floor　floor　floor

flower

[fláuər 플라우어]
명 꽃

flower　flower　flower　flower

fly [1]

[flai 플라이]
동 날다

fly　fly　fly　fly　fly

fly²

[flai 플라이]
명 파리

fly fly fly fly fly fly fly fly fly

follow

[fálou 팔로우]
동 따라가다

follow follow follow

food

[fu:d 푸-드]
명 음식

food food food food food food

fool

[fu:l 푸-울]
명 바보

fool fool fool fool fool fool fool

foolish

[fúːliʃ 푸-울리쉬]
형 어리석은

foolish foolish foolish foolish

foot

[fut 풋]
명 발

foot foot foot foot foot foot foot

football

[fútbɔ̀ːl 풋보-올]
명 축구

football football

for

[fɔːr 포-]
전 ～을 위해

for for for for for for for for

forehead

[fɔ́(:)rid 포리드]
명 이마

forehead　forehead

foreign

[fɔ́(:)rin 포린]
형 외국의

foreign　foreign　foreign　foreign

foreigner

[fɔ́(:)rinəːr 포리너–]
명 외국인

foreigner　foreigner　foreigner

forest

[fɔ́(:)rist 포리스트]
명 숲

forest　forest　forest　forest　forest

forget

[fərgét 퍼겟]
동 잊다

forget　forget　forget　forget　forget

fork

[fɔːrk 포-크]
명 포크

fork　fork　fork　fork　fork　fork　fork

forty

[fɔ́ːrti 포-티]
명 40, 마흔

forty　forty　forty　forty

four

[fɔːr 포-]
명 4, 넷

four　four　four　four　four　four

fourteen

[fɔ́:rtí:n 포-티-인]
(명) 14, 열 넷

fourteen fourteen fourteen fourteen

fox

[faks 팍스]
(명) 여우

fox fox fox fox

free

[fri: 프리-]
(형) 자유로운

free free free free free free

fresh

[freʃ 프레쉬]
(형) 새로운, 신선한

fresh fresh fresh fresh fresh

Friday

[fráidi 프라이디]
명 금요일

Friday Friday Friday Friday

friend

[frend 프렌드]
명 친구

friend friend friend

frog

[frɔːg 프로-그]
명 개구리

frog frog frog frog

from

[frʌm 프럼]
전 ~로부터

from from from from from from

front

[frʌnt 프런트]
명 앞(쪽)

front front front front front front

fruit

[fruːt 프루-트]
명 과일

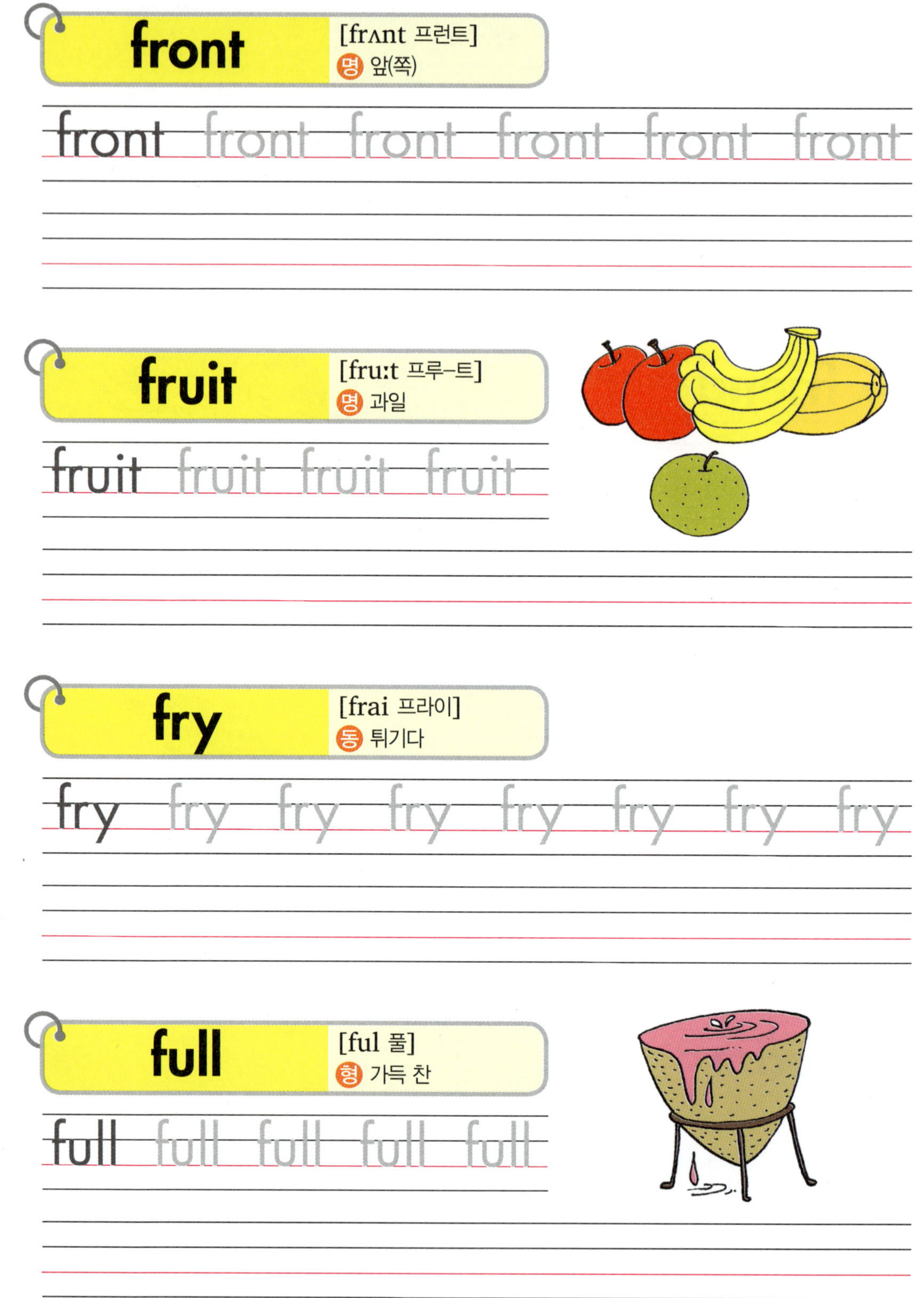

fruit fruit fruit fruit

fry

[frai 프라이]
동 튀기다

fry fry fry fry fry fry fry fry

full

[ful 풀]
형 가득 찬

full full full full full

fun

[fʌn 펀]
명 즐거운 생각

fun fun fun fun fun fun fun fun

funny

[fʌ́ni 퍼니]
형 재미있는

funny funny funny

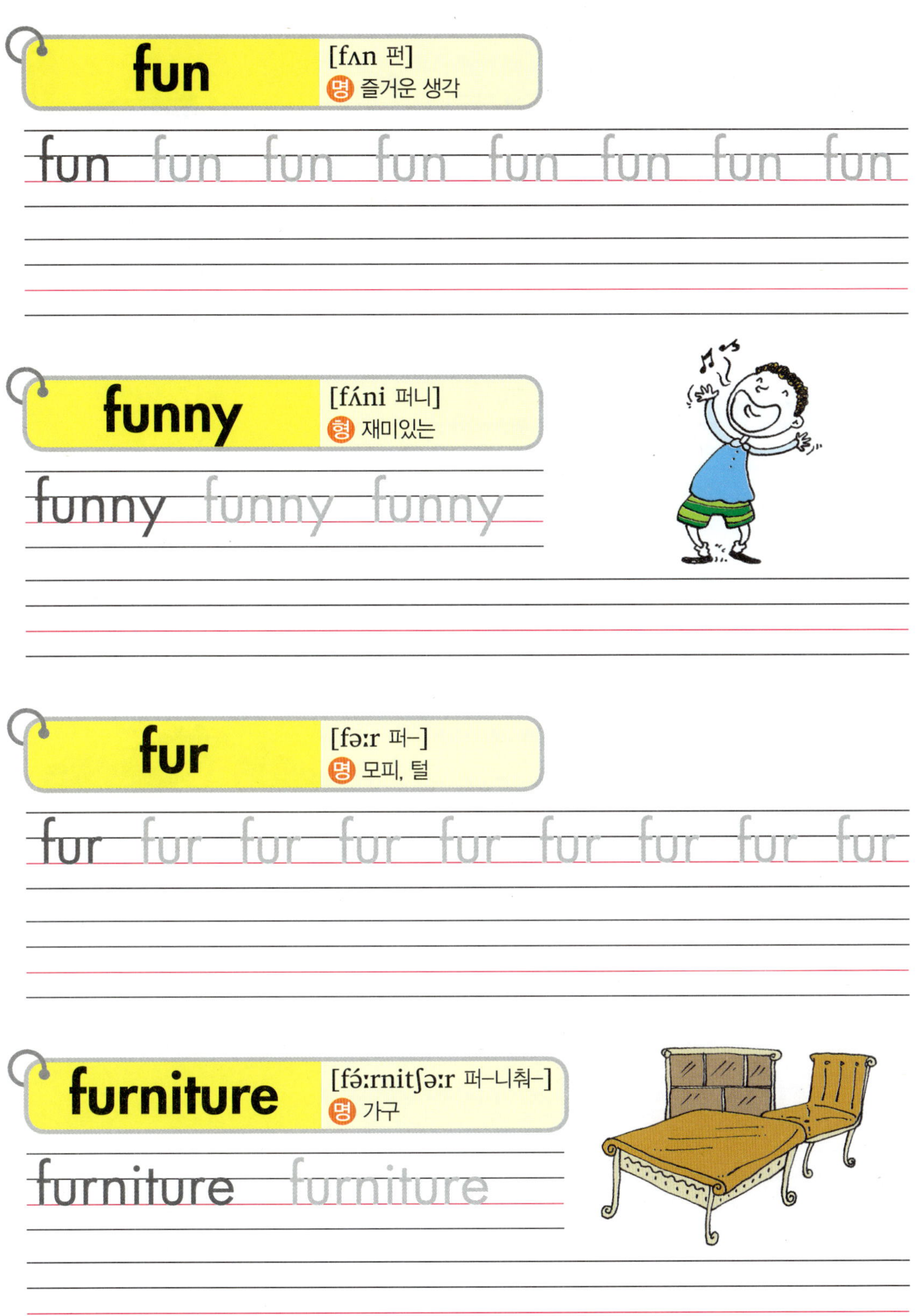

fur

[fəːr 퍼–]
명 모피, 털

fur fur fur fur fur fur fur fur fur

furniture

[fə́ːrnitʃəːr 퍼–니춰–]
명 가구

furniture furniture

Gg

game

[geim 게임]
명 놀이, 경기

game　game　game　game　game

garden

[gá:rdn 가-든]
명 정원, 마당

garden　　garden

gas

[gæs 개스]
명 가스

gas　gas　gas　gas　gas　gas　gas

gate

[geit 게이트]
명 문

gate　　gate　　gate　　gate　　gate　　gate

gentleman

[ʤéntlmən 쥄틀먼]
명 신사

gentleman

get

[get 겟]
동 얻다

get　　get　　get　　get　　get　　get　　get　　get

gift

[gift 기프트]
명 선물

gift　　gift　　gift　　gift

giraffe

giraffe · giraffe

girl

girl girl girl girl girl girl girl girl

give

give give give give

glad

glad glad glad glad glad glad glad

glass

[glæs 글래스]
명 유리(잔)

glass   glass   glass

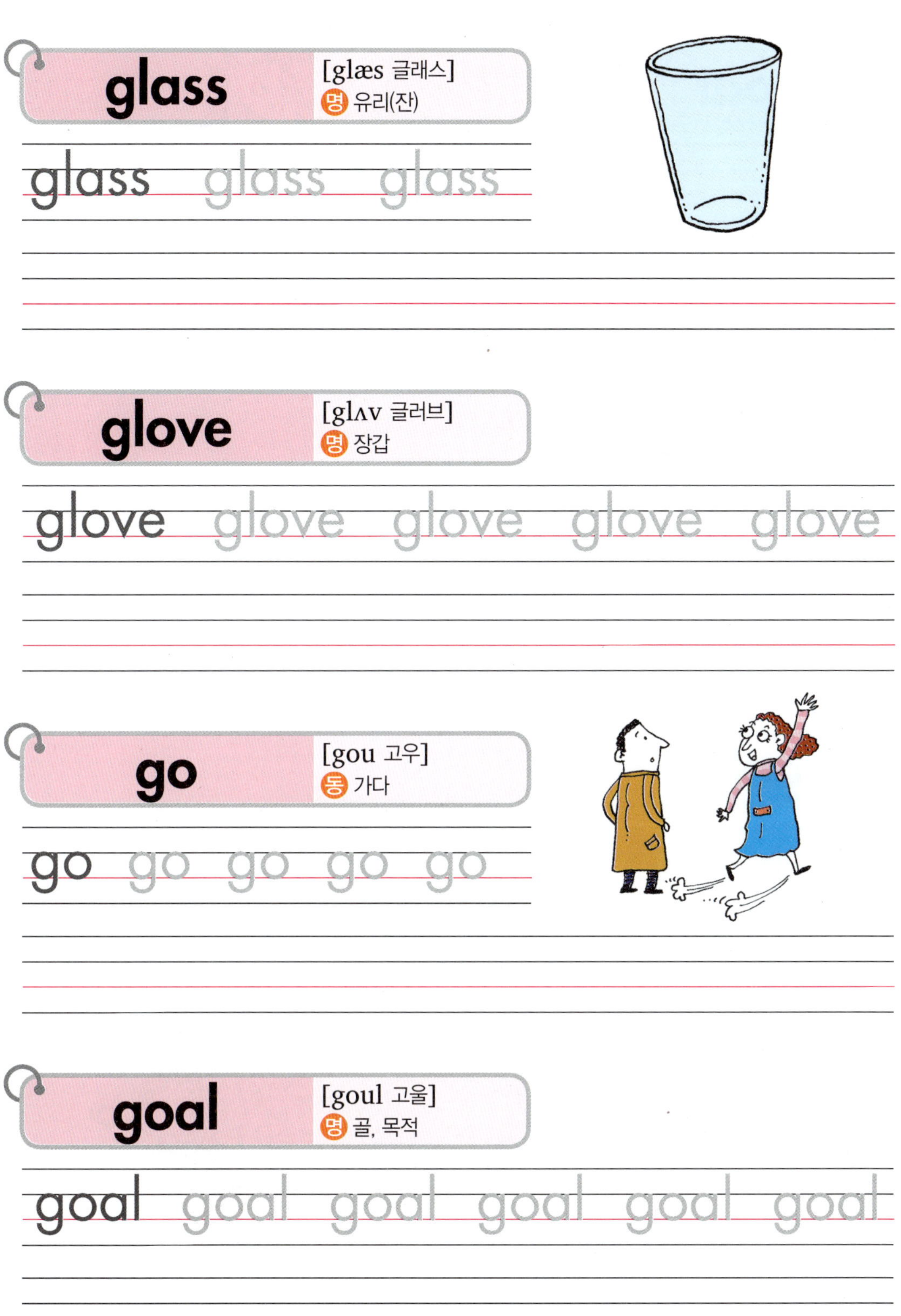

glove

[glʌv 글러브]
명 장갑

glove   glove   glove   glove   glove

go

[gou 고우]
동 가다

go go go go go

goal

[goul 고울]
명 골, 목적

goal goal goal goal goal goal

goat

[gout 고우트]
명 염소

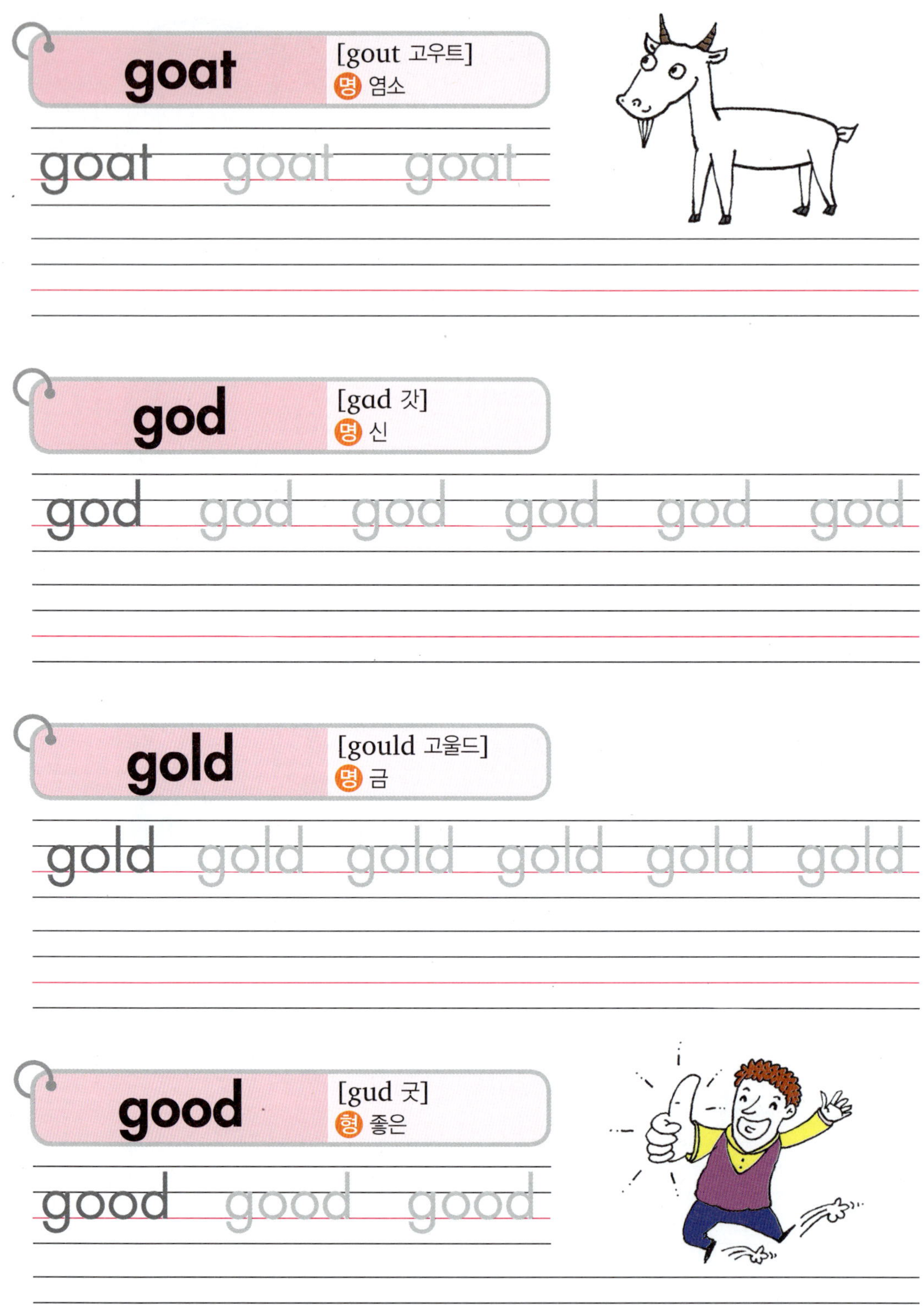

goat   goat   goat

god

[gad 갓]
명 신

god   god   god   god   god   god

gold

[gould 고울드]
명 금

gold   gold   gold   gold   gold   gold

good

[gud 굿]
형 좋은

good   good   good

goose

[gu:s 구-스]
명 거위

goose  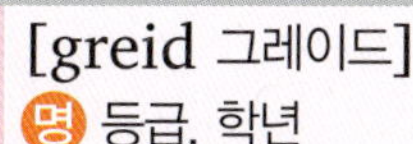

grade

[greid 그레이드]
명 등급, 학년

grade grade grade

grandfather

[grǽndfà:ðər 그랜드파-더]
명 할아버지

grandfather grandfather

grandmother

[grǽndmʌðər 그랜드머더]
명 할머니

grandmother grandmother

grape

[greip 그레이프]
명 포도

grape　　grape　　grape　　grape

grass

[græs 그래스]
명 풀

grass　　grass　　grass

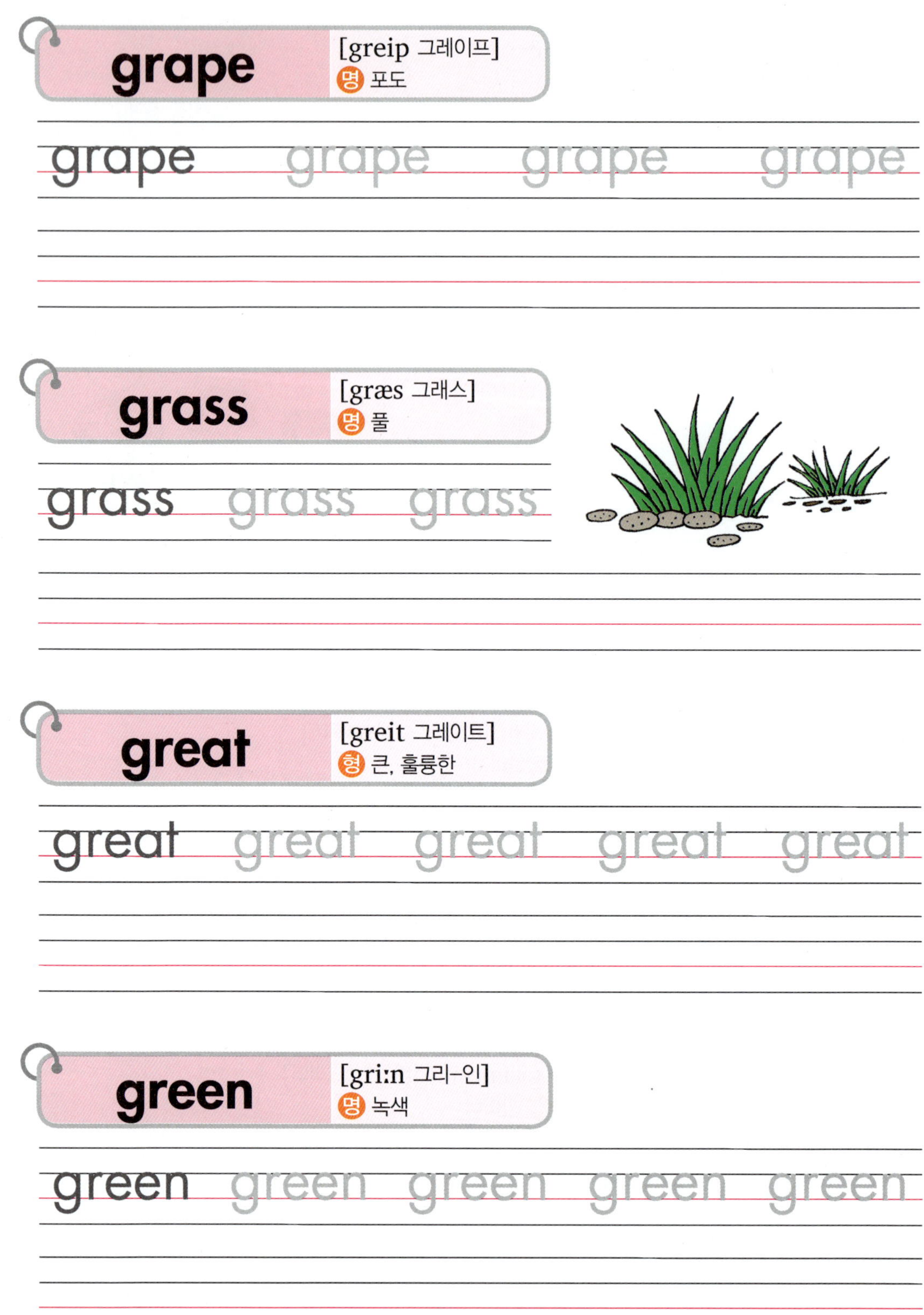

great

[greit 그레이트]
형 큰, 훌륭한

great　　great　　great　　great　　great

green

[gri:n 그리-인]
명 녹색

green　　green　　green　　green　　green

greeting

[grí:tiŋ 그리-팅]
명 인사

greeting   greeting

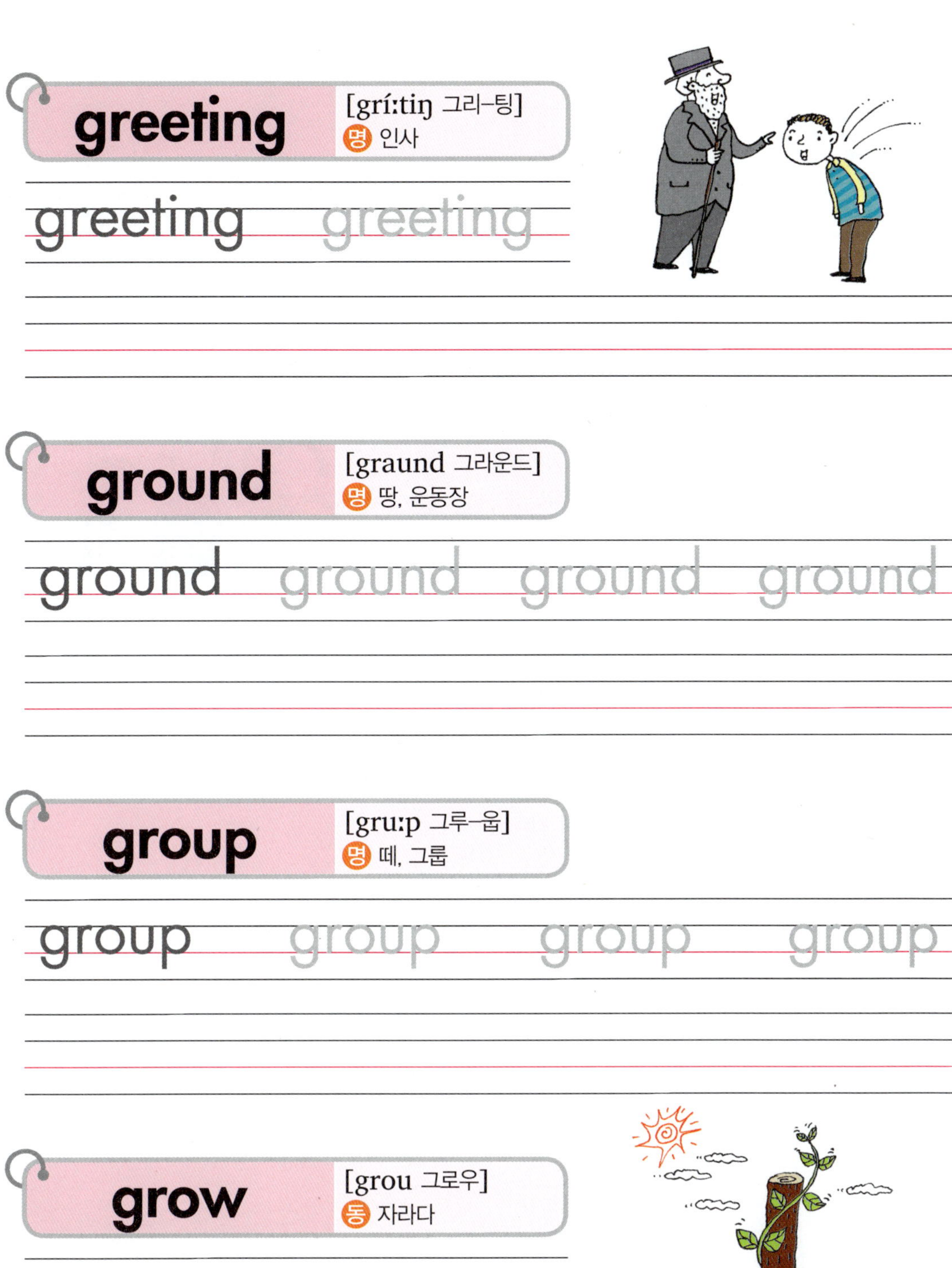

ground

[graund 그라운드]
명 땅, 운동장

ground   ground   ground   ground

group

[gru:p 그루-웁]
명 떼, 그룹

group   group   group   group

grow

[grou 그로우]
동 자라다

grow   grow   grow

guest

[gest 게스트]
명 손님

guest　guest　guest　guest　guest

guide

[gaid 가이드]
명 안내자

guide　guide　guide

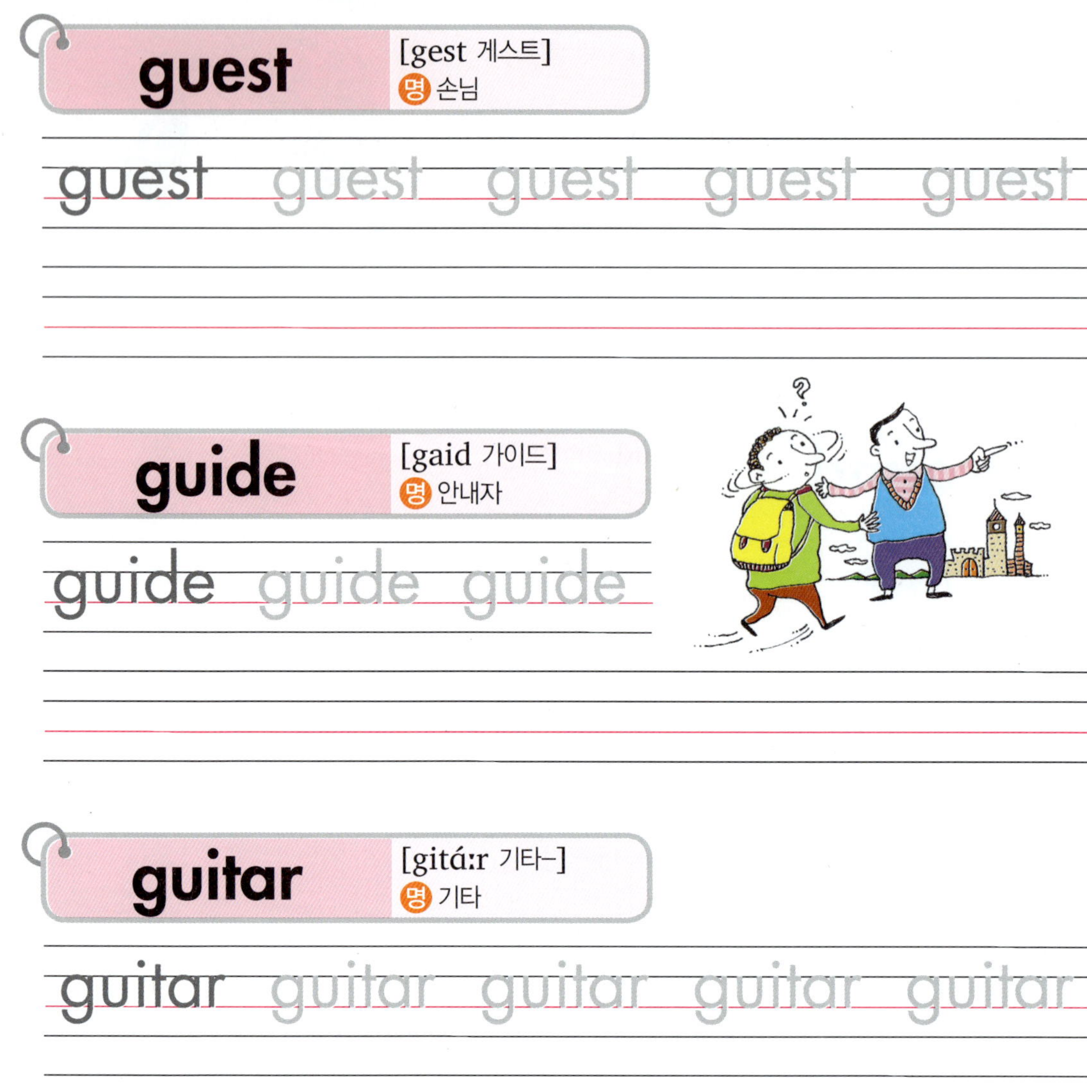

guitar

[gitá:r 기타–]
명 기타

guitar　guitar　guitar　guitar　guitar

S
a
B
A
P

Hh

hair
[hɛər 헤어]
명 머리카락

hair hair hair hair hair hair

half
[hæf 해프]
명 (절)반

half half half half

hall
[hɔːl 호―올]
명 홀, 강당

hall hall hall hall hall hall hall

hamburger

[hǽmbə̀ːrgər 햄버–거]
(명) 햄버거

hamburger　hamburger hamburger

hand

[hænd 핸드]
(명) 손

hand　hand　hand

handle

[hǽndl 핸들]
(명) 손잡이

handle　handle

handsome

[hǽnsəm 핸섬]
(형) (얼굴이)잘 생긴

handsome　handsome　handsome

hang

hang　hang　hang

happen

happen　happen　happen　happen

happy

happy　happy　happy　happy

hard

hard　hard　hard

hat
[hæt 햇]
명 (테가 있는)모자

hat hat hat hat hat hat hat hat

hate
[heit 헤이트]
동 싫어하다

hate hate hate hate

have
[hæv 해브]
동 가지다

have have have have have

head
[hed 헷]
명 머리

head head head

health

[helθ 헬쓰]
명 건강

health　health　health　health

hear

[hiər 히어]
동 듣다

hear hear hear hear

heart

[haːrt 하—트]
명 가슴, 마음

heart　heart　heart　heart　heart

heavy

[hévi 헤비]
형 무거운

heavy heavy heavy

helicopter

[hélikàptər 헬리캅터]
명 헬리콥터

helicopter　helicopter　helicopter

hello

[helóu 헬로우]
감 여보세요!

hello　hello　hello　hello　hello

help

[help 헬프]
동 돕다

help help help help

hen

[hen 헨]
명 암탉

hen hen hen hen hen hen hen

here
[hiər 히어]
부 여기에

here here here here

hero
[híːrou 히-로우]
명 영웅

hero hero hero hero hero hero

hide
[haid 하이드]
동 숨기다, 숨다

hide hide hide hide

high
[hai 하이]
형 높은

high high high high high high high

hiking

hiking hiking hiking

hill

hill hill hill hill hill hill hill hill

history

history history history history

hit

hit hit hit hit hit

hold

[hould 호울드]
동 잡다

hold　hold　hold　hold　hold　hold

hole

[houl 호울]
명 구멍

hole hole hole hole

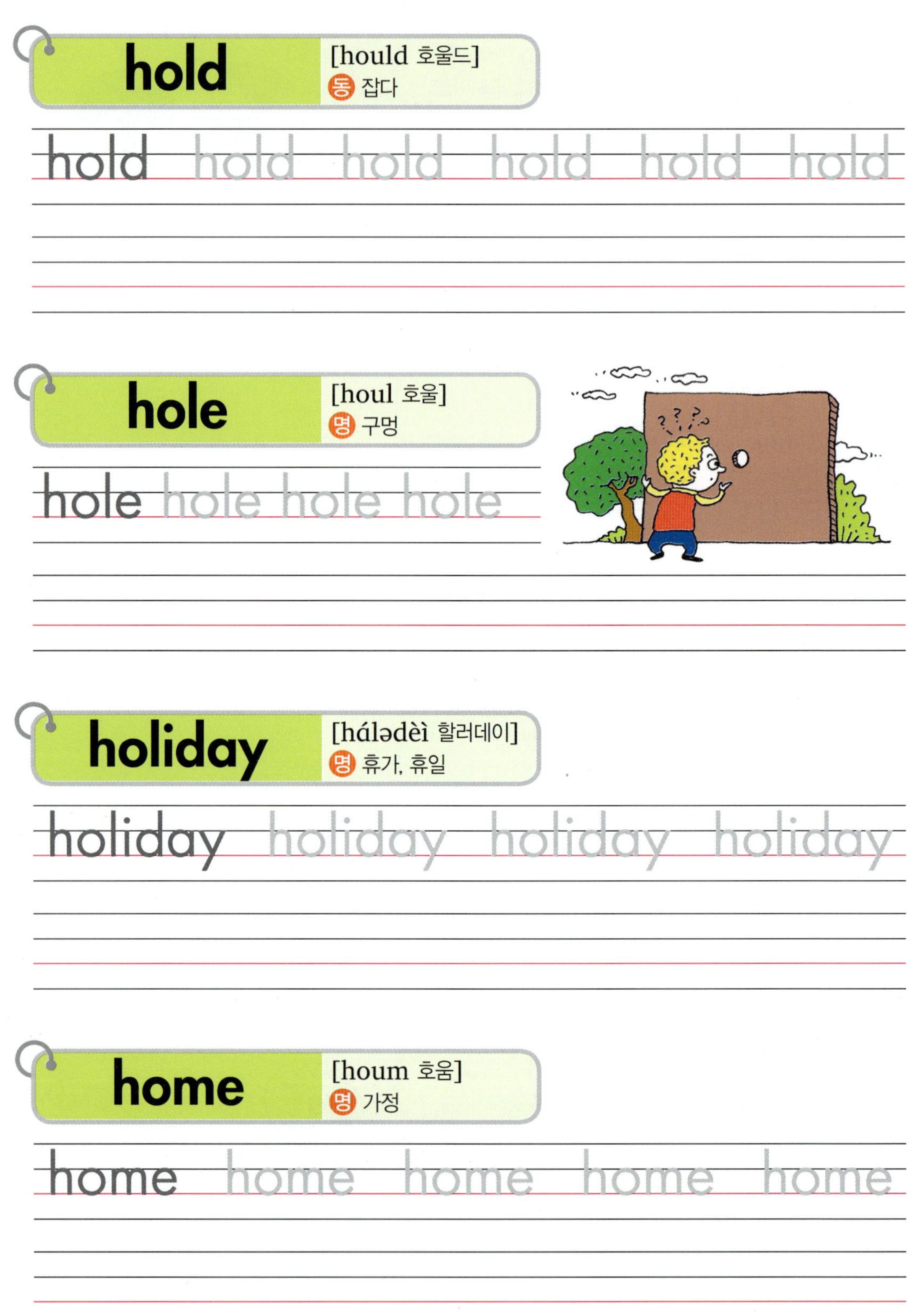

holiday

[hálədèi 할러데이]
명 휴가, 휴일

holiday　holiday　holiday　holiday

home

[houm 호움]
명 가정

home　home　home　home　home

homework [houmwèrk 호움웍]
명 숙제

homework　homework　homework

hope [houp 호우프]
명 희망

hope　hope　hope　hope　hope

horse [hɔːrs 호-스]
명 말

horse　horse　horse　horse　horse

hospital [háspitl 하스피틀]
명 병원

hospital　hospital

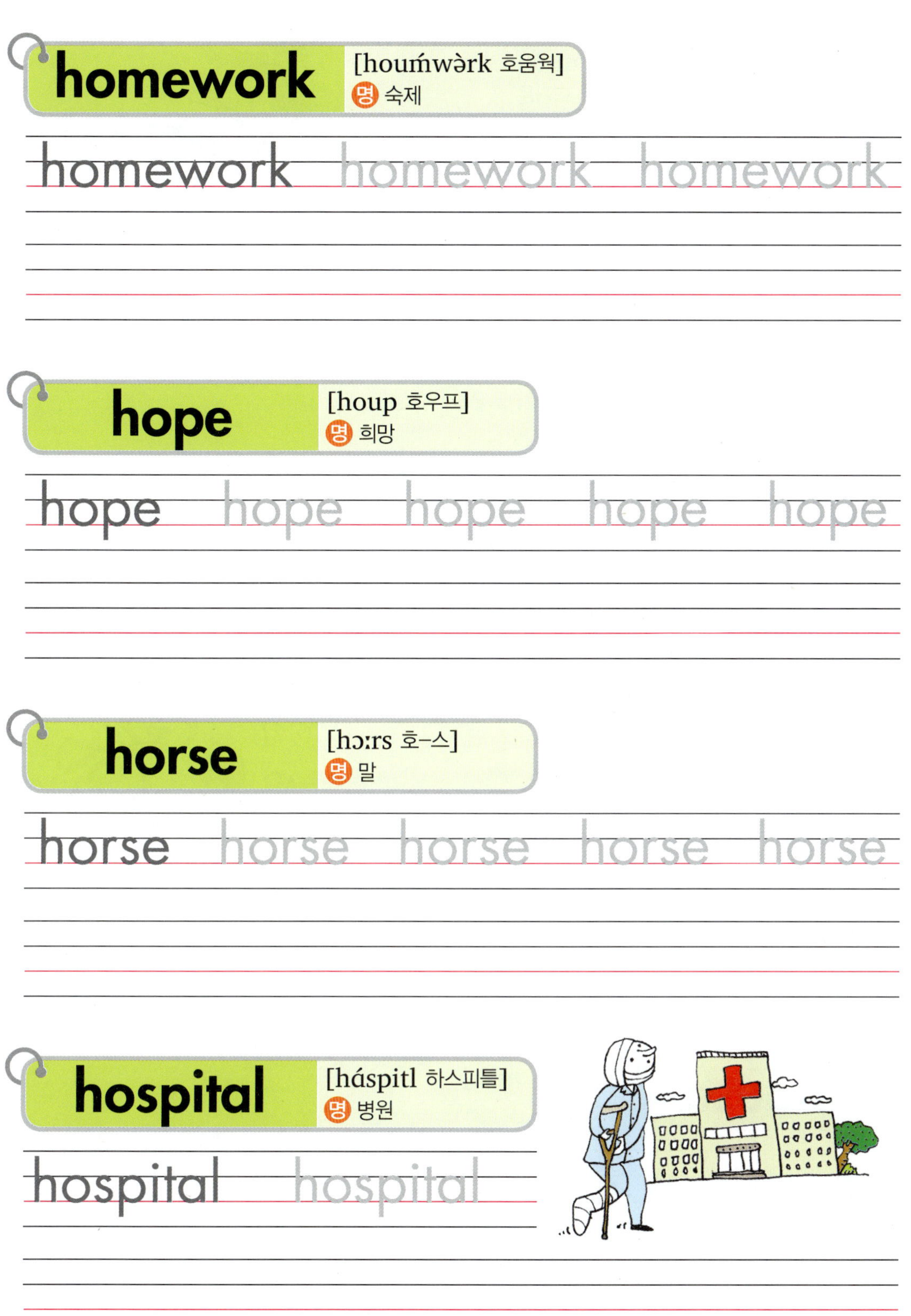

hot
[hat 핫]
형 뜨거운

hot hot hot hot

hotel
[houtél 호우텔]
명 호텔, 여관

hotel hotel hotel hotel hotel

hour
[áuər 아우어]
명 시간, 시각

hour hour hour hour

house
[haus 하우스]
명 집

house house house house house

hundred

[hʌ́ndrəd 헌드럿]
명 백, 100

hundred hundred hundred hundred

hungry

[hʌ́ŋgri 헝그리]
형 배고픈

hungry hungry

hurry

[hə́:ri 허–리]
동 서두르다

hurry hurry hurry hurry hurry

hurt

[hə:rt 허–트]
동 상처 내다, 아프다

hurt hurt hurt hurt hurt hurt hurt

husband

[hʌ́zbənd 허즈번드]
명 남편

husband　husband

Ii

ice
[ais 아이스]
명 얼음

ice ice ice ice ice ice ice ice

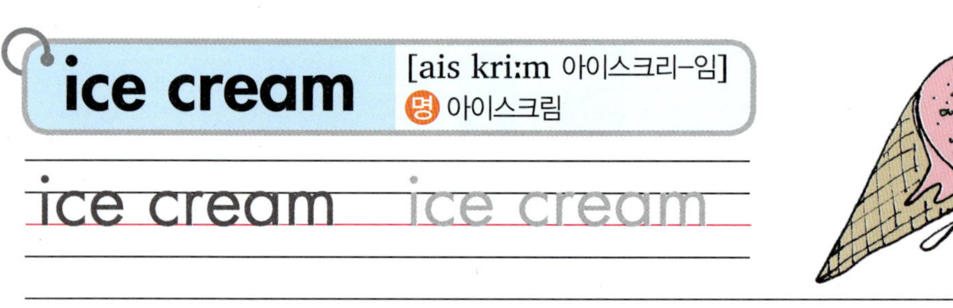

ice cream
[ais kri:m 아이스크리–임]
명 아이스크림

ice cream　ice cream

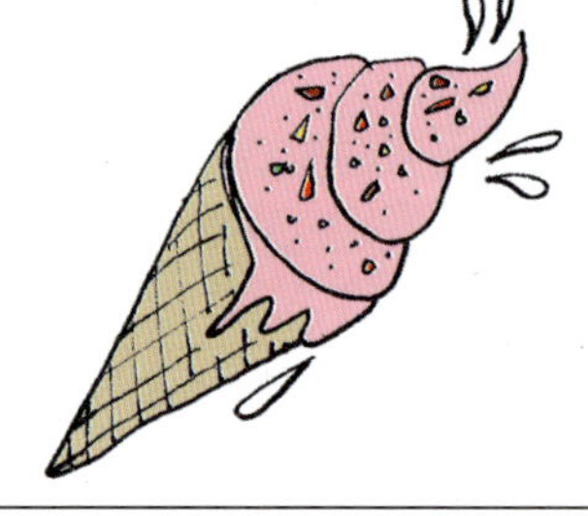

idea
[aidíːə 아이디–어]
명 생각

idea idea idea idea idea idea

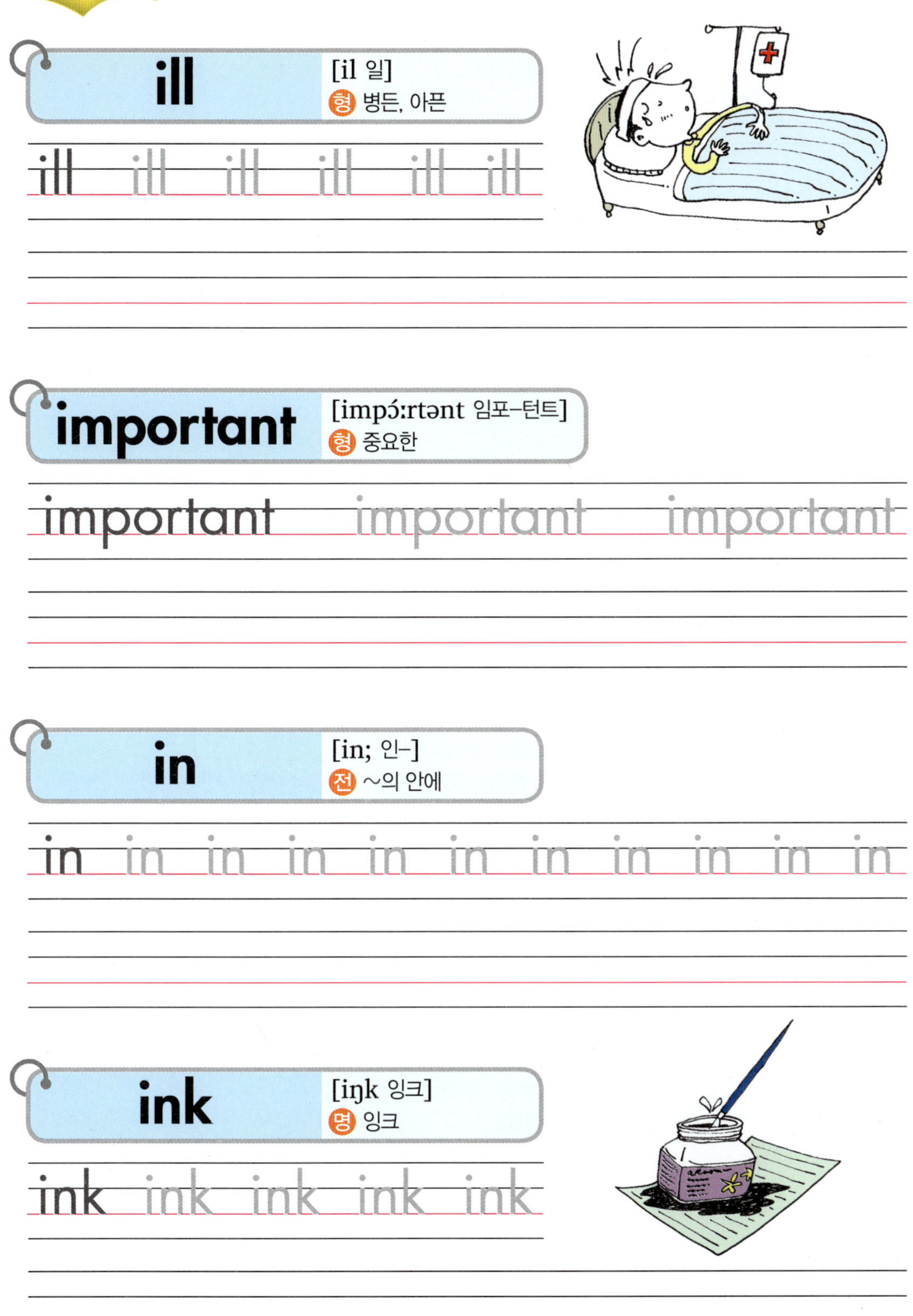

ill

[il 일]
형 병든, 아픈

ill　ill　ill　ill　ill　ill

important

[impɔ́ːrtənt 임포–턴트]
형 중요한

important　important　important

in

[in; 인–]
전 ～의 안에

in　in　in　in　in　in　in　in　in　in　in

ink

[iŋk 잉크]
명 잉크

ink　ink　ink　ink　ink

inside

[ínsáid 인사이드]
명 안쪽

inside inside inside inside inside

instead

[instéd 인스텟]
부 그 대신에

instead instead instead instead

interest

[íntərist 인터리스트]
명 관심, 흥미

interest interest

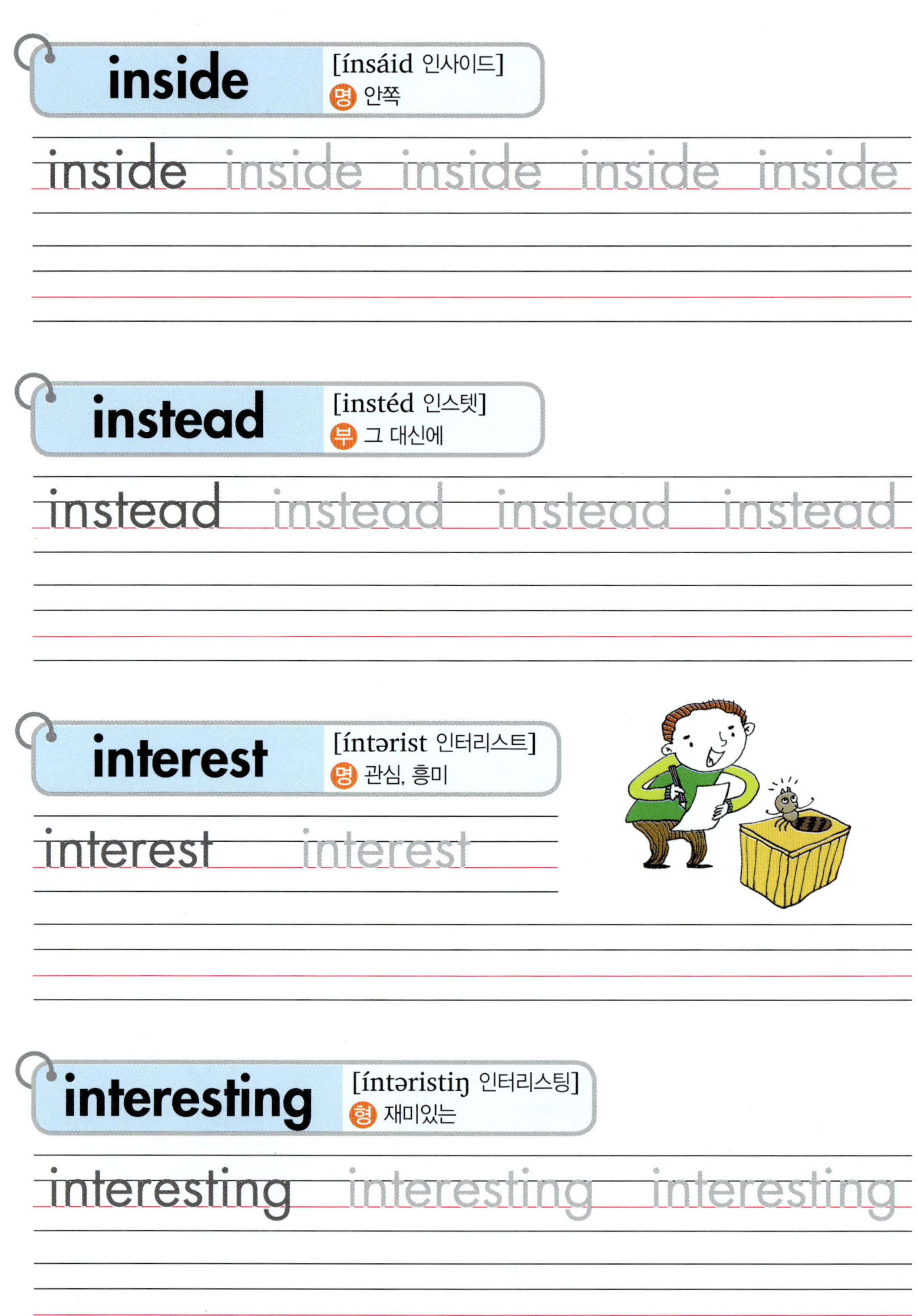

interesting

[íntəristiŋ 인터리스팅]
형 재미있는

interesting interesting interesting

into

[íntu 인투]
전 ~안으로

into into into into into into into

introduce

[ìntrədjúːs 인트러듀-스]
동 소개하다

introduce introduce

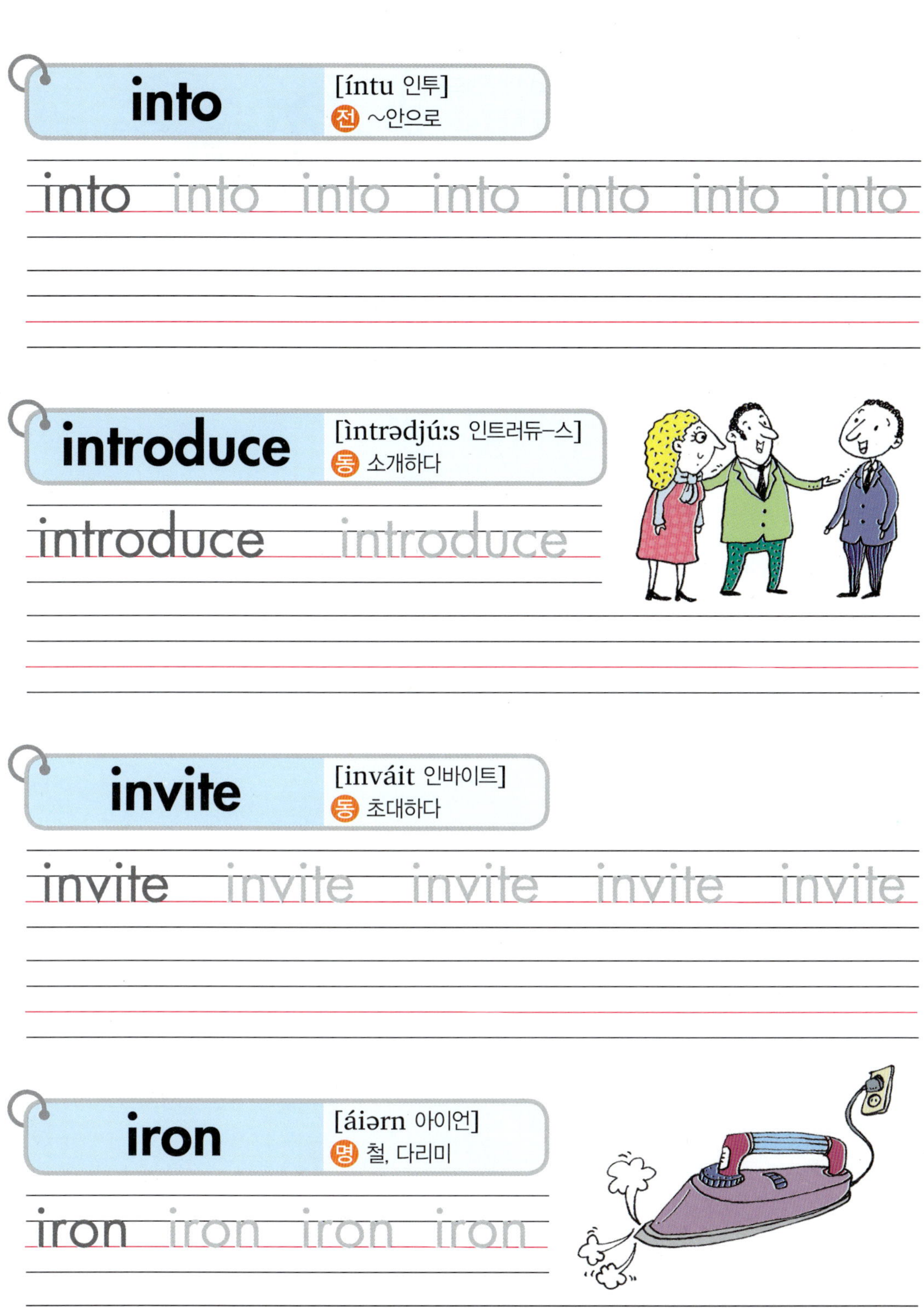

invite

[inváit 인바이트]
동 초대하다

invite invite invite invite invite

iron

[áiərn 아이언]
명 철, 다리미

iron iron iron iron

island

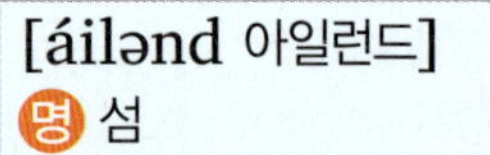

[áilənd 아일런드]
명 섬

island island island

Jj

jacket

[dʒǽkit 재킷]
명 재킷, 웃옷

jacket jacket jacket

jam

[dʒæm 잼]
명 잼

jam jam jam jam jam jam jam

January

[dʒǽnjuèri 재뉴에리]
명 1월

January January January January

job

[dʒab 좝]
명 일

job　job　job　job

join

[dʒɔin 조인]
동 합류하다

join　join　join　join　join　join　join

journey

[dʒə́:rni 줘-니]
명 여행

journey　journey　journey　journey

joy

[dʒɔi 조이]
명 기쁨

joy　joy　joy　joy　joy

juice

[dʒuːs 쥬-스]
명 주스

juice　juice　juice

July

[dʒuːlái 쥬-울라이]
명 7월

July　July　July　July　July　July　July

jump

[dʒʌmp 점프]
동 뛰어오르다

jump　jump　jump

June

[dʒuːn 쥬-운]
명 6월

June　June　June　June　June　June

jungle

[dʒʌ́ŋgl 정글]
명 밀림

jungle　jungle　jungle　jungle

just

[dʒʌst 줘스트]
부 이제방금, 바로

just　just　just　just

Kk

kangaroo
[kæ̀ŋgərúː 캥거루–]
명 캥거루

kangaroo   kangaroo   kangaroo

keep
[kiːp 키–입]
동 계속하다

keep   keep   keep   keep   keep

key
[kiː 키–]
명 열쇠

key   key   key   key

kick

[kik 킥]
동 차다

kick　kick　kick　kick

kid

[kid 킷]
명 아이

kid　kid　kid　kid　kid

kill

[kil 킬]
동 죽이다

kill　kill　kill　kill　kill　kill　kill　kill

kilometer

[kilámitər 킬라미터]
명 킬로미터

kilometer　kilometer　kilometer

kind¹

[kaind 카인드]
형 친절한

kind　kind　kind　kind　kind　kind

kind²

[kaind 카인드]
명 종류

kind kind kind kind

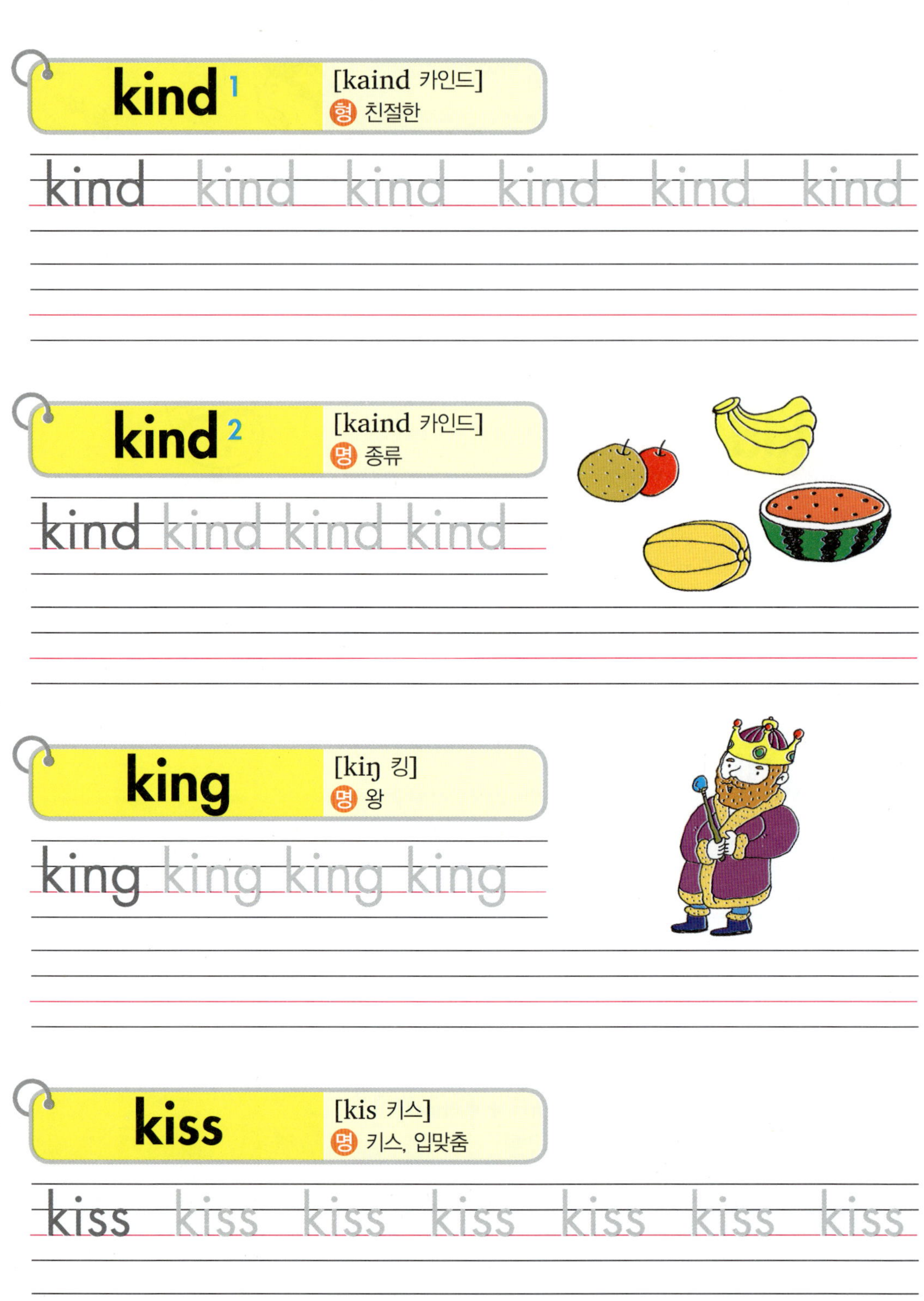

king

[kiŋ 킹]
명 왕

king king king king

kiss

[kis 키스]
명 키스, 입맞춤

kiss　kiss　kiss　kiss　kiss　kiss　kiss

kitchen

[kítʃin 키췬]
명 부엌

kitchen kitchen kitchen kitchen

knee

[ni: 니—]
명 무릎

knee knee knee

knife

[naif 나이프]
명 칼

knife knife knife knife knife

knock

[nak 낙]
동 두드리다

knock knock knock

know

[nou 노우]
동 알다

know know know

koala

[kouá:lə 코우아―알러]
명 코알라

koala koala koala koala koala

lady
[léidi 레이디]
명 숙녀

lady　lady　lady　lady　lady　lady

lake
[leik 레이크]
명 호수

lake　lake　lake　lake　lake　lake

lamp
[læmp 램프]
명 등불

lamp　lamp　lamp

land

[lænd 랜드]
명 땅, 육지

land　land　land　land　land　land

large

[lɑːrdʒ 라-쥐]
형 큰, 넓은

large　large　large　large　large

last

[læst 래스트]
형 맨 마지막의

last　last　last　last

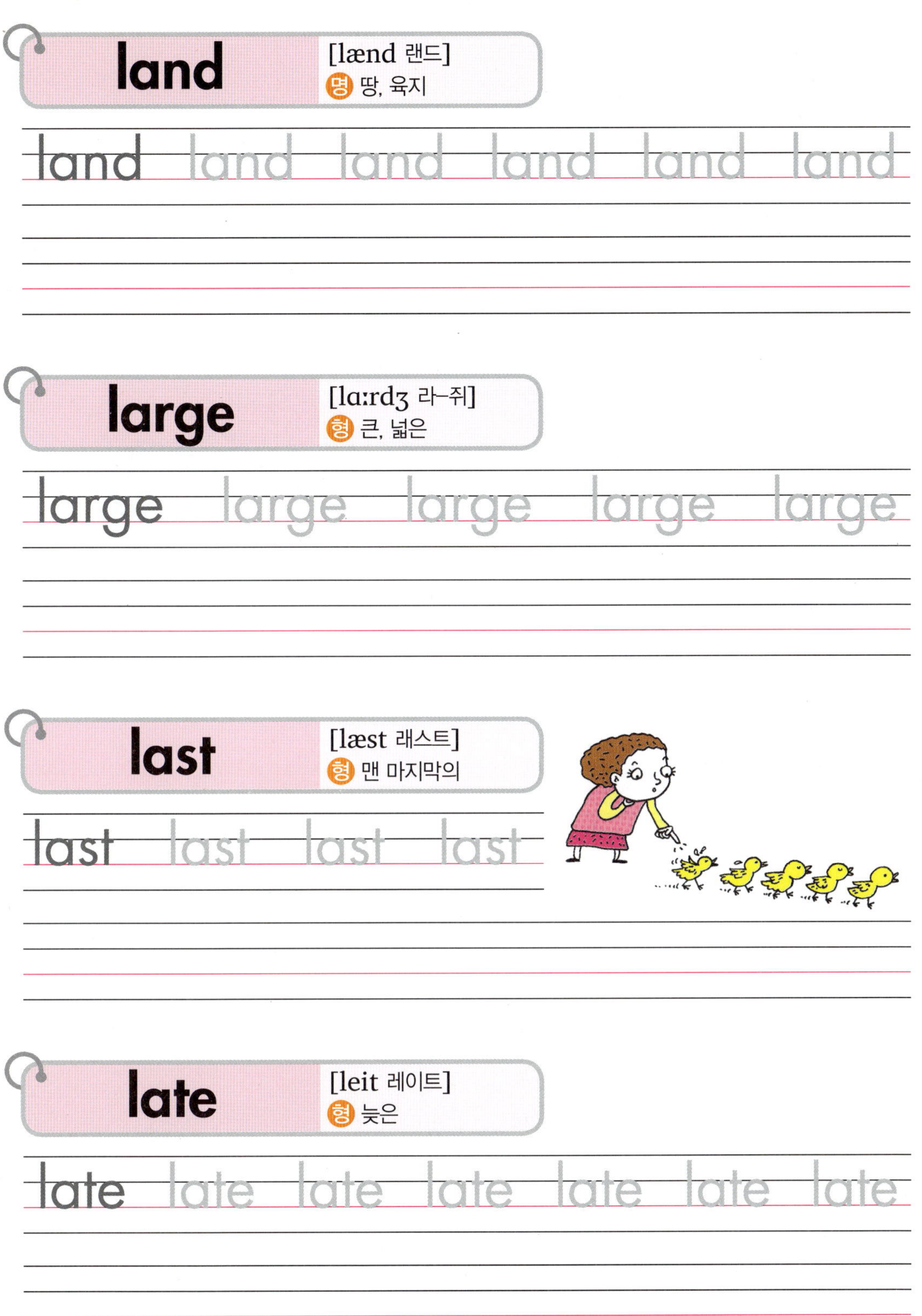

late

[leit 레이트]
형 늦은

late　late　late　late　late　late　late

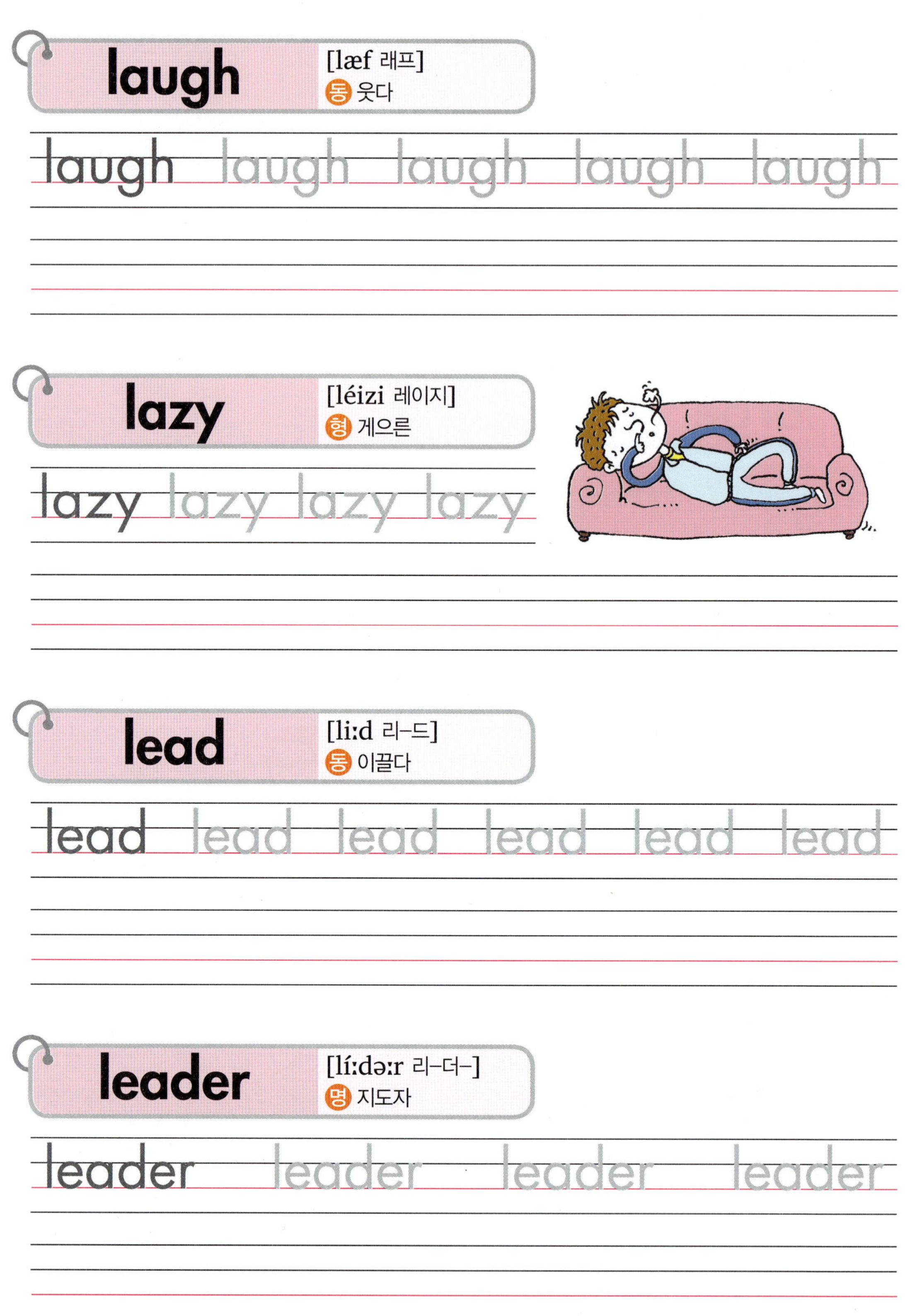

laugh
[læf 래프]
동 웃다

laugh laugh laugh laugh laugh

lazy
[léizi 레이지]
형 게으른

lazy lazy lazy lazy

lead
[li:d 리-드]
동 이끌다

lead lead lead lead lead lead

leader
[lí:dər 리-더-]
명 지도자

leader leader leader leader

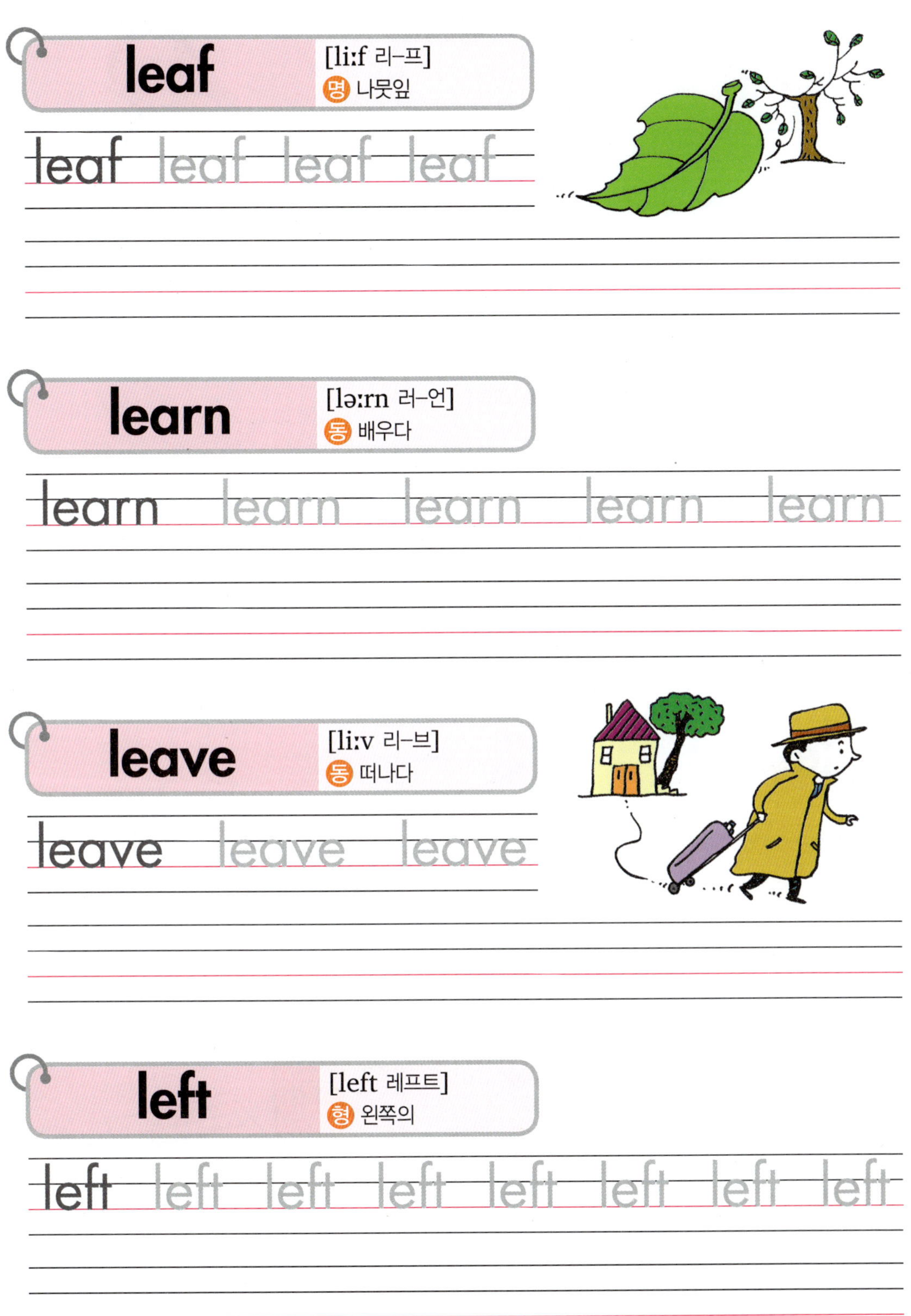

leaf

[li:f 리-프]
명 나뭇잎

leaf leaf leaf leaf

learn

[lə:rn 러-언]
동 배우다

learn learn learn learn learn

leave

[li:v 리-브]
동 떠나다

leave leave leave

left

[left 레프트]
형 왼쪽의

left left left left left left left left

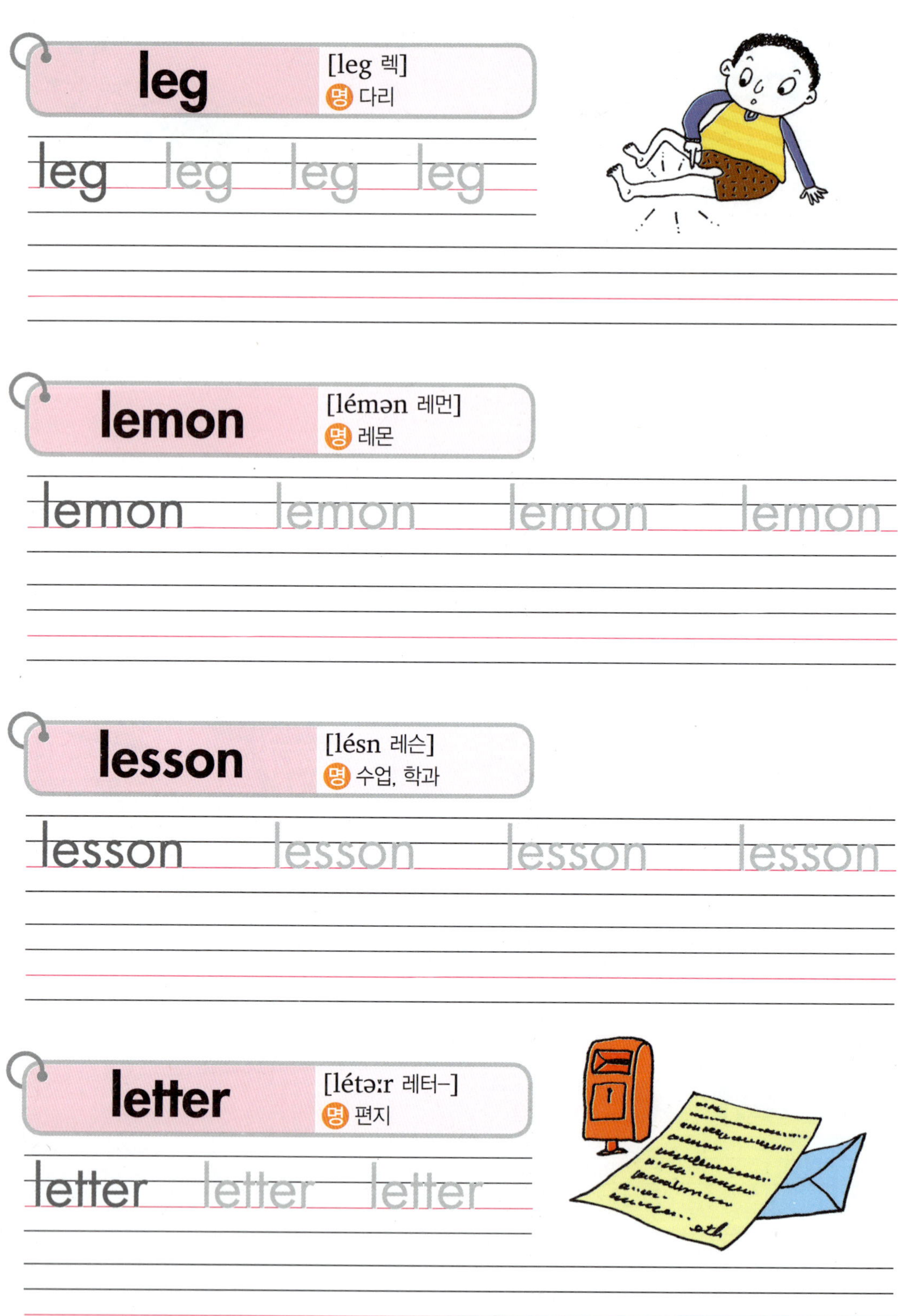

leg
[leg 렉]
명 다리

leg leg leg leg

lemon
[lémən 레먼]
명 레몬

lemon lemon lemon lemon

lesson
[lésn 레슨]
명 수업, 학과

lesson lesson lesson lesson

letter
[létəːr 레터-]
명 편지

letter letter letter

library

[láibrèri 라이브레리]
명 도서관

library　library　library　library

lie

[lai 라이]
명 거짓말

lie　lie　lie　lie　lie

life

[laif 라이프]
명 생명, 생활

life　life　life　life　life　life　life　life

light

[lait 라이트]
명 빛

light　light　light　light　light　light

like
[laik 라이크]
동 좋아하다

like　like　like　like

lily
[líli 릴리]
명 나리, 백합

lily　lily　lily　lily　lily　lily　lily　lily

lion
[láiən 라이언]
명 사자

lion　lion　lion　lion　lion　lion　lion

lip
[lip 립]
명 입술

lip　lip　lip　lip　lip

listen

[lísən 리슨]
동 듣다

listen listen listen listen listen

little

[[lítl 리틀]
형 작은

little little little little

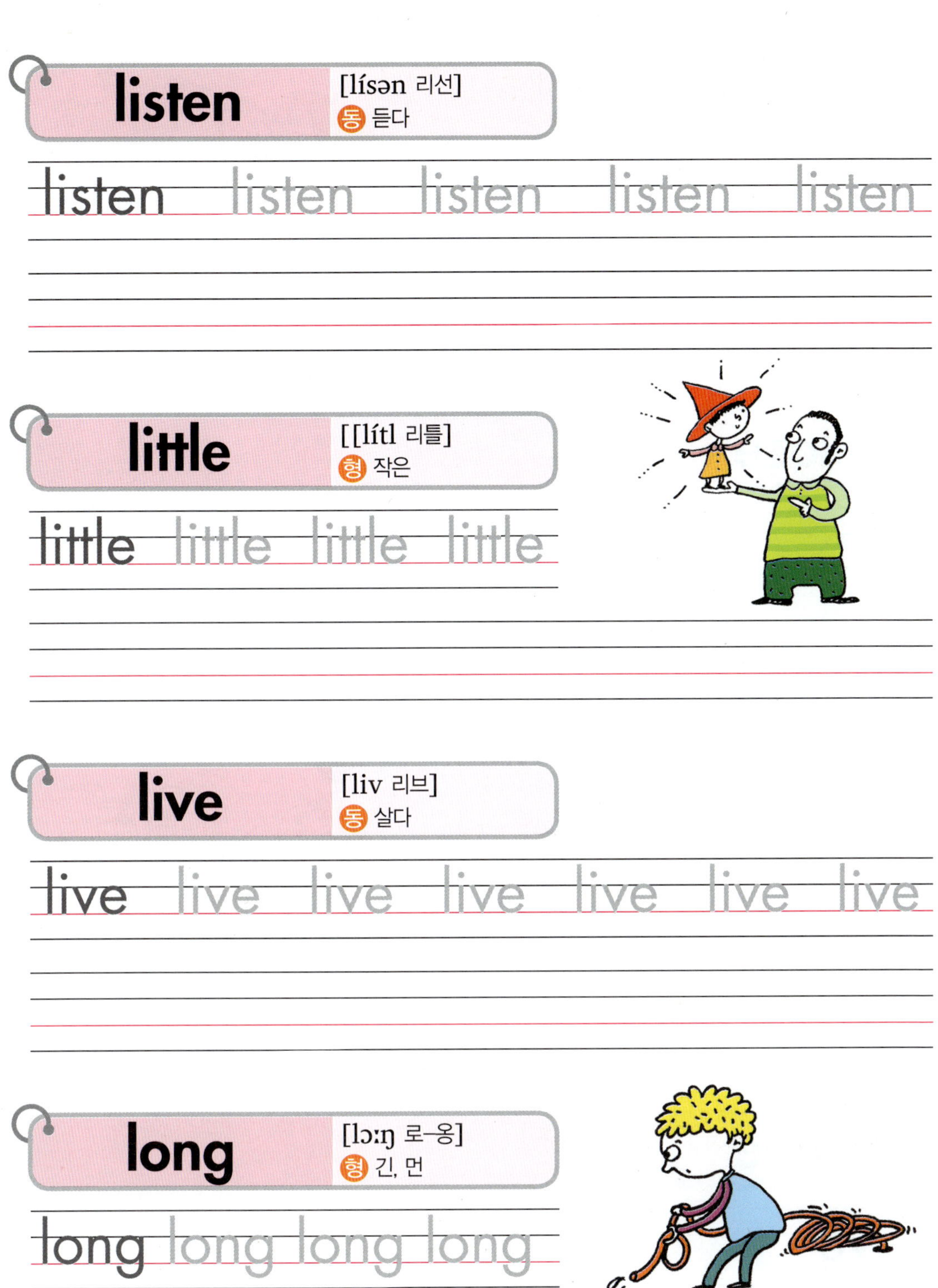

live

[liv 리브]
동 살다

live live live live live live live

long

[lɔːŋ 로-옹]
형 긴, 먼

long long long long

look

[luk 룩]
동 보다

look look look look

lose

[luːz 루-즈]
동 잃다

lose lose lose lose lose lose

loud

[laud 라우드]
형 시끄러운

loud loud loud loud

love

[lʌv 러브]
명 사랑

love love love love love love

low

[lou 로우]
형 낮은

low　low　low　low

lucky

[lʌ́ki 러키]
형 행운의

lucky　lucky　lucky　lucky　lucky

lunch

[lʌntʃ 런취]
명 점심

lunch　lunch　lunch　lunch　lunch

Mm

ma'am [mæ(:)m 맴]
명 마님, 아주머니

ma'am   ma'am   ma'am   ma'am

machine [məʃíːn 머쉬–인]
명 기계

machine   machine

mad [mæd 맷]
형 미친, 화난

mad   mad   mad   mad   mad   mad

magic

[mædʒik 매직]
명 마법

magic magic magic

mail

[meil 메일]
명 우편물

mail mail mail mail mail mail

make

[meik 메이크]
동 만들다

make make make make make

man

[mæn 맨]
명 남자, 인간

man man man man

manner
[mǽnəːr 매너–]
명 방법, 예절

manner　manner　manner　manner

many
[méni 메니]
형 많은(셀 수 있는 명사)

many　many　many

map
[mæp 맵]
명 지도

map　map　map　map

March
[maːrtʃ 마–취]
명 3월

March　March　March　March

march

[mɑːrtʃ 마-취]
명 행진

march march march

---

market

[mɑ́ːrkit 마-킷]
명 시장

market market market market

---

marry

[mǽri 매리]
동 결혼하다

marry marry marry marry

---

mask

[mæsk 매스크]
명 탈, 복면

mask mask mask

match

[mætʃ 매취]
명 성냥, 시합

match match match

May

[mei 메이]
명 5월

May May May May May May

may

[mei 메이]
조 ~할(일)지도 모른다

may may may may may may

maybe

[méibi 메이비]
부 어쩌면, 아마

maybe maybe

meal

[mi:l 미-일]
명 식사

meal   meal   meal   meal   meal

mean

[mi:n 미-인]
동 의미하다

mean   mean   mean   mean   mean

meat

[mi:t 미-트]
명 고기

meat   meat   meat

meet

[mi:t 미-트]
동 만나다

meet   meet   meet

member

[mémbər 멤버]
명 일원, 회원

member　member member member

memory

[méməri 메머리]
명 기억

memory　memory

merchant

[mə́:rtʃənt 머-췬트]
명 상인

merchant　merchant　merchant

merry

[méri 메리]
형 명랑한, 즐거운

merry　merry　merry

message

[mésidʒ 메시쥐]
명 메시지, 소식

message　　message　　message

middle

[mídl 미들]
명 중앙, 한 가운데

middle　　middle

milk

[milk 밀크]
명 우유

milk　milk　milk　milk

million

[míljən 밀리언]
명 백만

million　　million　　million　　million

mind

[maind 마인드]
명 마음

mind　mind　mind　mind　mind

minute

[mínit 미닛]
명 (시간의)분

minute　minute　minute　minute

mirror

[mírər 미러]
명 거울

mirror mirror mirror

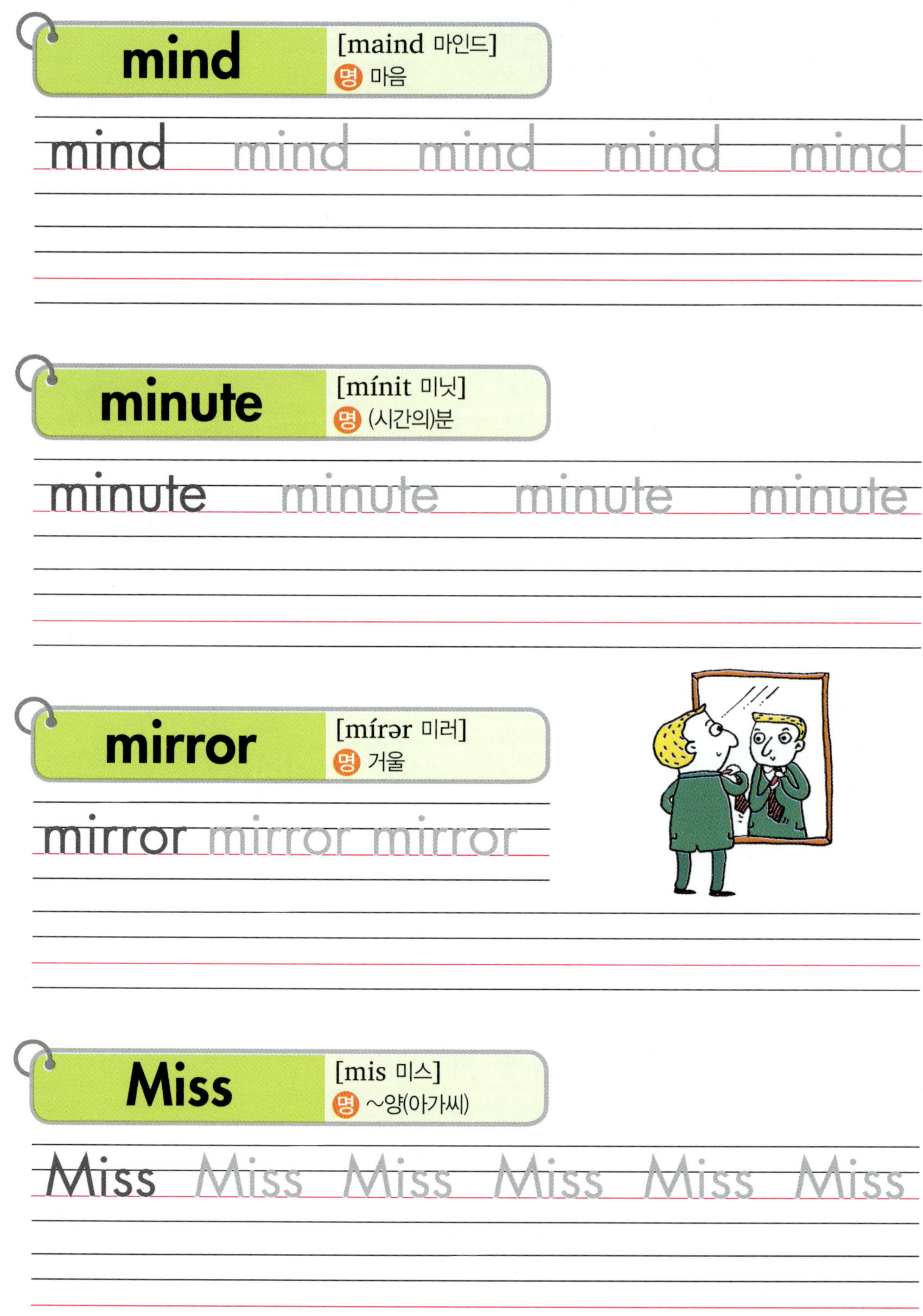

Miss

[mis 미스]
명 ～양(아가씨)

Miss　Miss　Miss　Miss　Miss　Miss

miss

[mis 미스]
동 놓치다, 잡지 못하다

miss miss miss miss

mistake

[mistéik 미스테이크]
명 잘못

mistake mistake mistake mistake

mix

[miks 믹스]
동 섞다

mix mix mix mix

model

[mádl 마들]
명 모델, 본보기

model model model model

moment

[móumənt 모우먼트]
명 순간

moment moment moment moment

Monday

[mʌ́ndi 먼디]
명 월요일

Monday   Monday   Monday

money

[mʌ́ni 머니]
명 돈

money   money

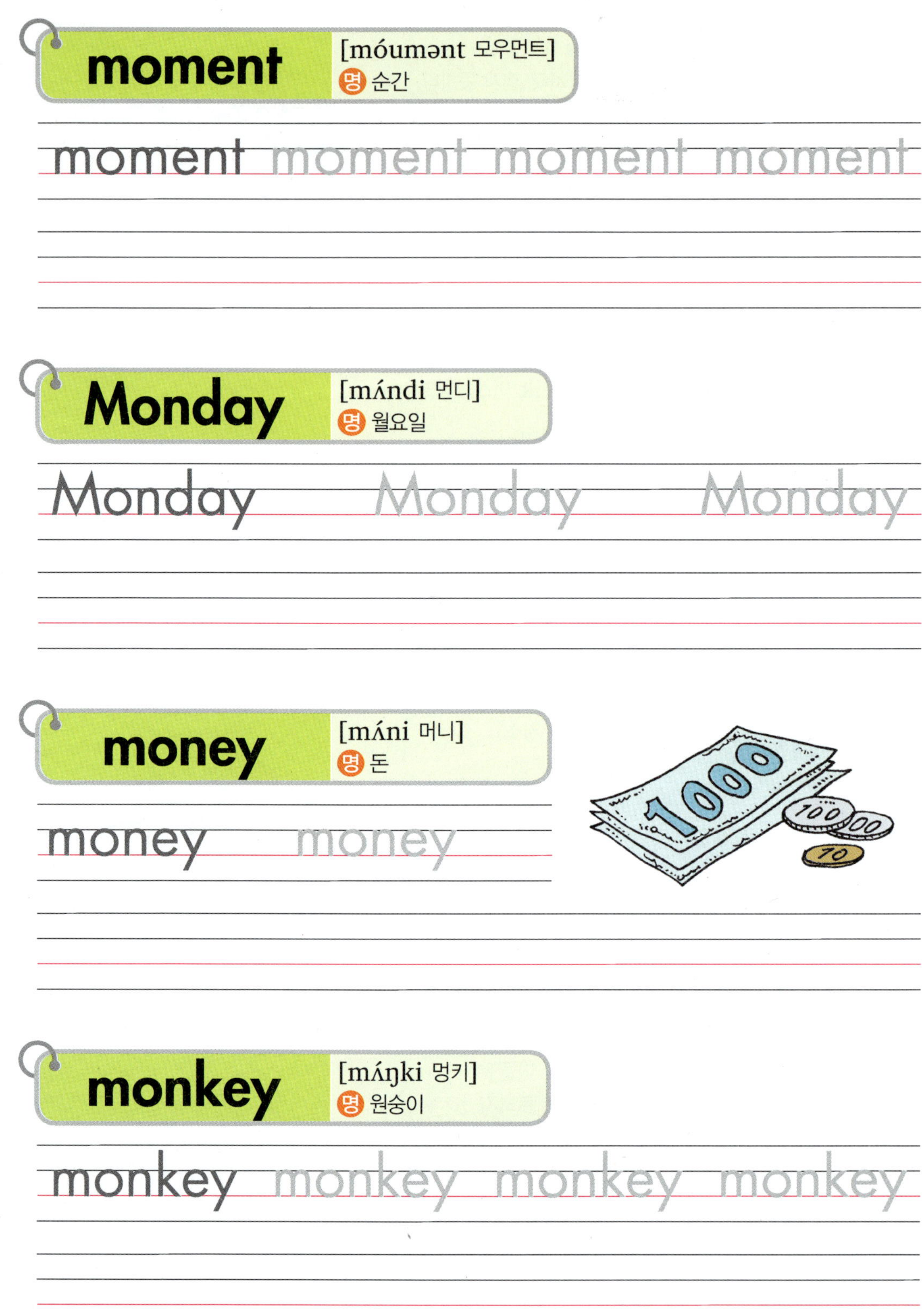

monkey

[mʌ́ŋki 멍키]
명 원숭이

monkey monkey monkey monkey

month

[mʌnθ 먼쓰]
명 (한)달

month　month　month　month　month

moon

[muːn 무-운]
명 (천체)달

moon　moon　moon　moon　moon

more

[mɔːr 모-]
형 더 많은, 더 큰

more　more　more

morning

[mɔ́ːrniŋ 모-닝]
명 아침, 오전

morning　morning

mother

[mʌ́ðəːr 머더-]
명 어머니

mother   mother   mother   mother

mountain

[máunt-ən 마운트-언]
명 산

mountain   mountain

mouse

[maus 마우스]
명 생쥐

mouse   mouse

mouth

[mauθ 마우쓰]
명 입

mouth   mouth   mouth   mouth   mouth

move

[mu:v 무-브]
동 움직이다

move　move　move

movie

[mú:vi 무-비]
명 영화

movie　movie　movie　movie　movie

Mr.

[místə:r 미스터-]
명 ～씨, ～님

Mr.　Mr.　Mr.　Mr.　Mr.　Mr.

Mrs.

[mísiz 미시즈]
명 ～부인, ～여사

Mrs.　Mrs.　Mrs.

much

[mʌtʃ 머취]
형 많은(셀 수 없는 명사)

much   much   much   much   much

museum

[mjuːzíːəm 뮤-지-엄]
명 박물관

museum   museum   museum   museum

music

[mjúːzik 뮤-직]
명 음악

music   music   music

S
R
Q
A
M

Nn

name [neim 네임]
명 이름

name　name　name　name　name

narrow [nǽrou 내로우]
형 (폭이) 좁은

narrow　narrow

nation [néiʃən 네이션]
명 국민, 국가

nation　nation　nation　nation　nation

near

[niər 니어]
부 가까이

near near near near near near

neck

[nek 넥]
명 목

neck neck neck

need

[ni:d 니—드]
동 필요하다

need need need need eed need

neighbor

[néibər 네이버]
명 이웃(사람)

neighbor neighbor neighbor

never

[névə:r 네버ㅡ]
부 결코 ～하지 않다

never　never　never　never　never

new

[nju: 뉴ㅡ]
형 새로운

new　new　new　new

news

[nju:z 뉴ㅡ즈]
명 뉴스, 보도

news　news　news　news　news

newspaper

[njú:zpèipə:r 뉴ㅡ즈페이퍼ㅡ]
명 신문(지)

newspaper　newspaper　newspaper

next

[nekst 넥스트]
형 다음의

next next next next next next

nice

[nais 나이스]
형 좋은, 친절한

nice nice nice nice nice nice

night

[nait 나이트]
명 밤

night night night

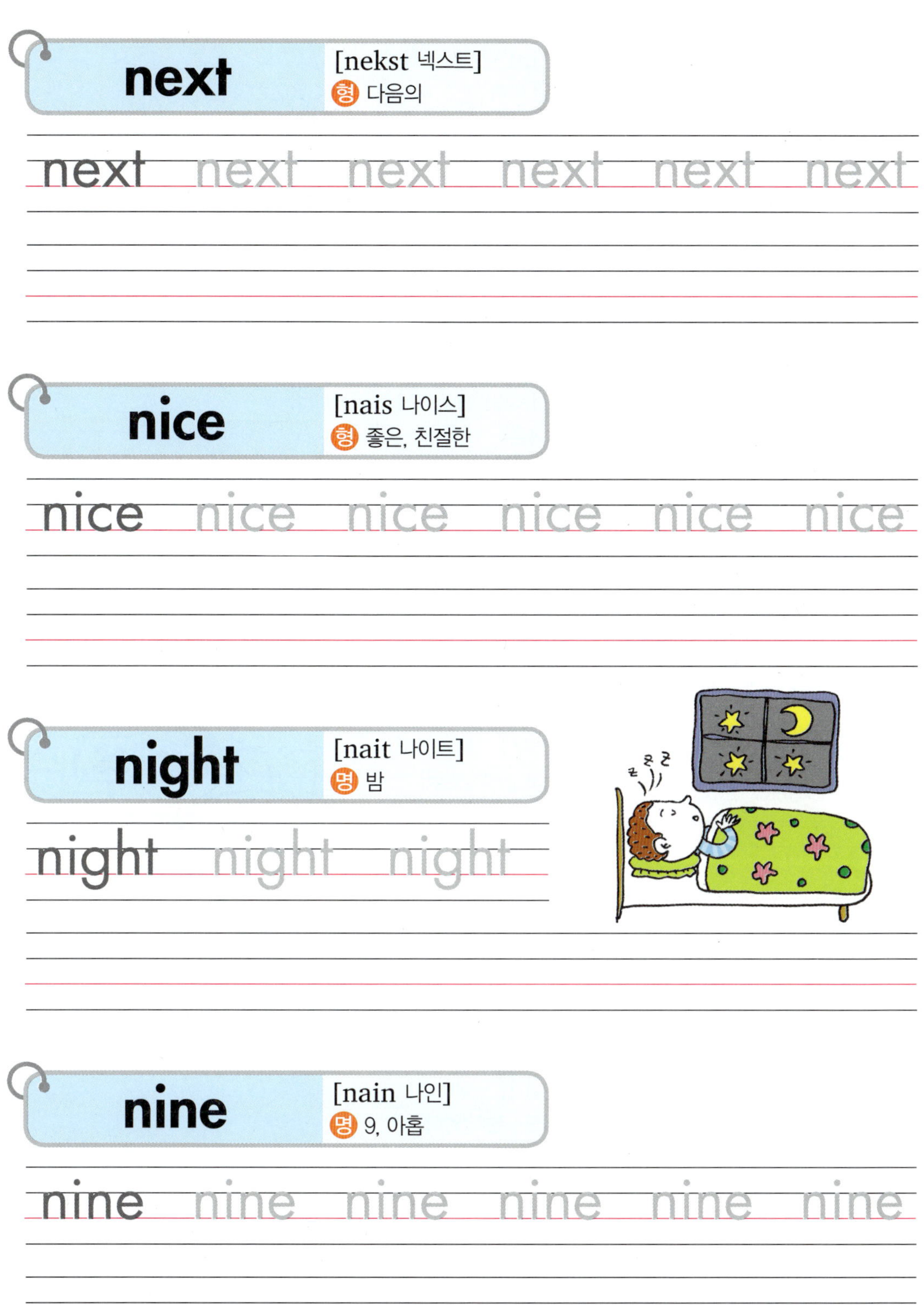

nine

[nain 나인]
명 9, 아홉

nine nine nine nine nine nine

nineteen

[náintí:n 나인티-인]
몡 19, 열 아홉

nineteen   nineteen   nineteen

ninety

[náinti 나인티]
몡 90, 아흔

ninety   ninety   ninety   ninety   ninety

no

[nou 노우]
몡 아니오(yes의 반대)

no   no   no   no   no

nobody

[nóubàdi 노우바디]
대 아무도– 않다(없다)

nobody   nobody   nobody   nobody

noise

[nɔiz 노이즈]
명 시끄러운 소리

noise   noise   noise

noon

[nuːn 누-운]
명 정오

noon   noon   noon   noon   noon

north

[nɔːrθ 노-쓰]
명 북(쪽)

north   north   north   north   north

nose

[nouz 노즈]
명 코

nose   nose   nose

not

[nat 낫]
부 ~아니다, 않다

not not not not not not not not

notebook

[nóutbùk 노우트북]
명 노트, 공책

notebook notebook

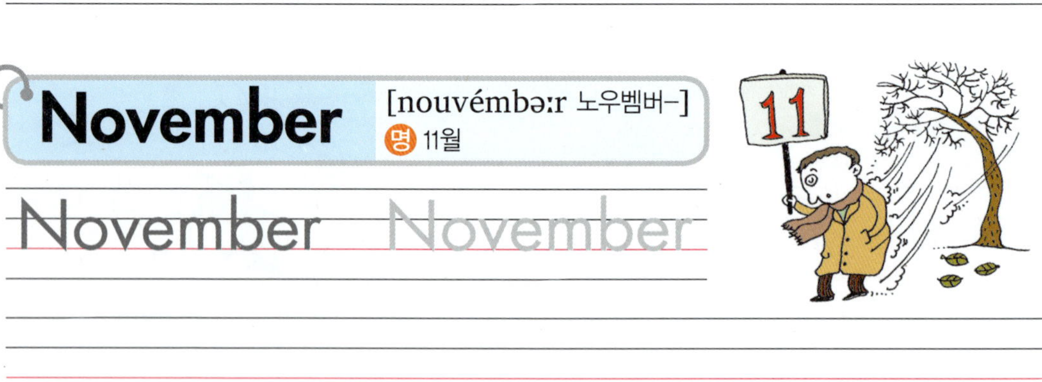

nothing

[nʌ́θiŋ 너씽]
대 아무 것[아무 일]도 —아님

nothing nothing nothing nothing

November

[nouvémbəːr 노우벰버ー]
명 11월

November November

now

[nau 나우]
부 지금, 현재

now　now　now　now　now　now

number

[nÁmbə:r 넘버-]
명 수, 숫자, 번호

number　number

nurse

[nə:rs 너-스]
명 간호사

nurse　nurse　nurse　nurse　nurse

ocean
[óuʃən 오우션]
명 대양, 해양

ocean   ocean   ocean   ocean

o'clock
[əklák 어클락]
부 ~시

o'clock   o'clock   o'clock   o'clock

October
[aktóubər 악토우버]
명 10월

October   October

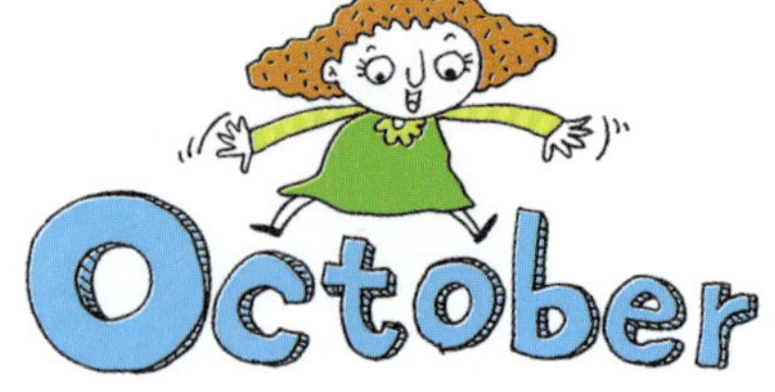

of
[əv 어브]
전 ~의, ~중의

of of of of of of of of of of of

off
[ɔf 오프]
부 떨어져, 멀리

off off off off off

office
[ɔ́(ː)fis 오피스]
명 사무실

office office office office office

often
[ɔ́ftən 아프턴]
부 자주, 종종

often often often often often often

oil

[ɔil 오일]
명 기름

oil oil oil oil oil oil oil oil oil

old

[ould 오울드]
형 나이 먹은, 낡은

old old old old

on

[ɑn 안]
전 ~위에

on on on on on

once

[wʌns 원스]
부 한 번, 이전에

once once once once once once once

one

[wʌn 원]
명 1, 하나

one　one　one　one

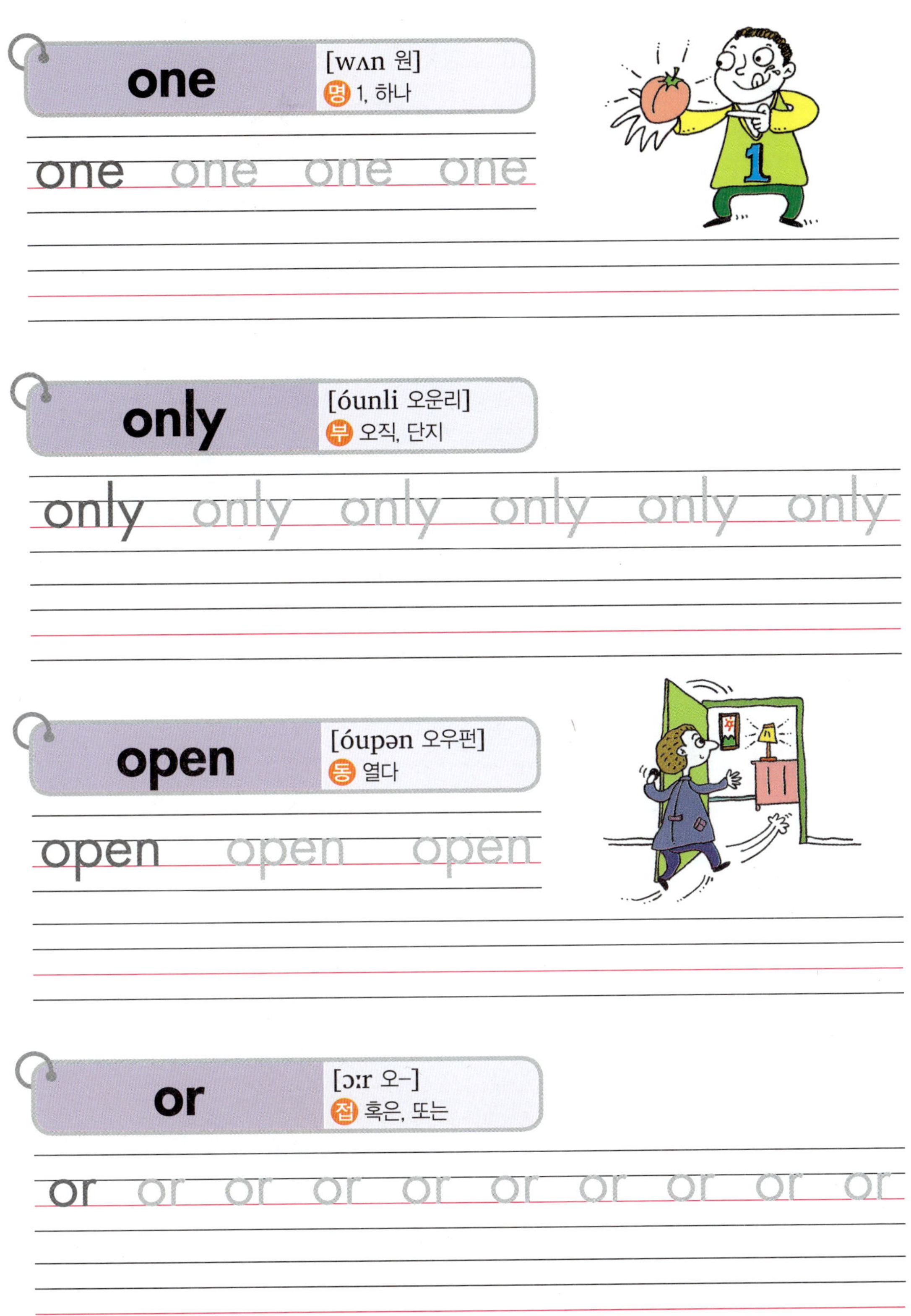

only

[óunli 오운리]
부 오직, 단지

only　only　only　only　only　only

open

[óupən 오우펀]
동 열다

open　open　open

or

[ɔːr 오-]
접 혹은, 또는

or　or　or　or　or　or　or　or　or　or

orange

[ɔ́(ː)rindʒ 오린쥐]
명 오렌지

orange   orange   orange   orange

order

[ɔ́ːrdər 오-더]
명 명령, 주문, 순서

order   order   order

organ

[ɔ́ːrgən 오-건]
명 오르간

organ   organ   organ   organ   organ

other

[ʌ́ðər 어더]
형 다른, 그 밖의

other   other   other

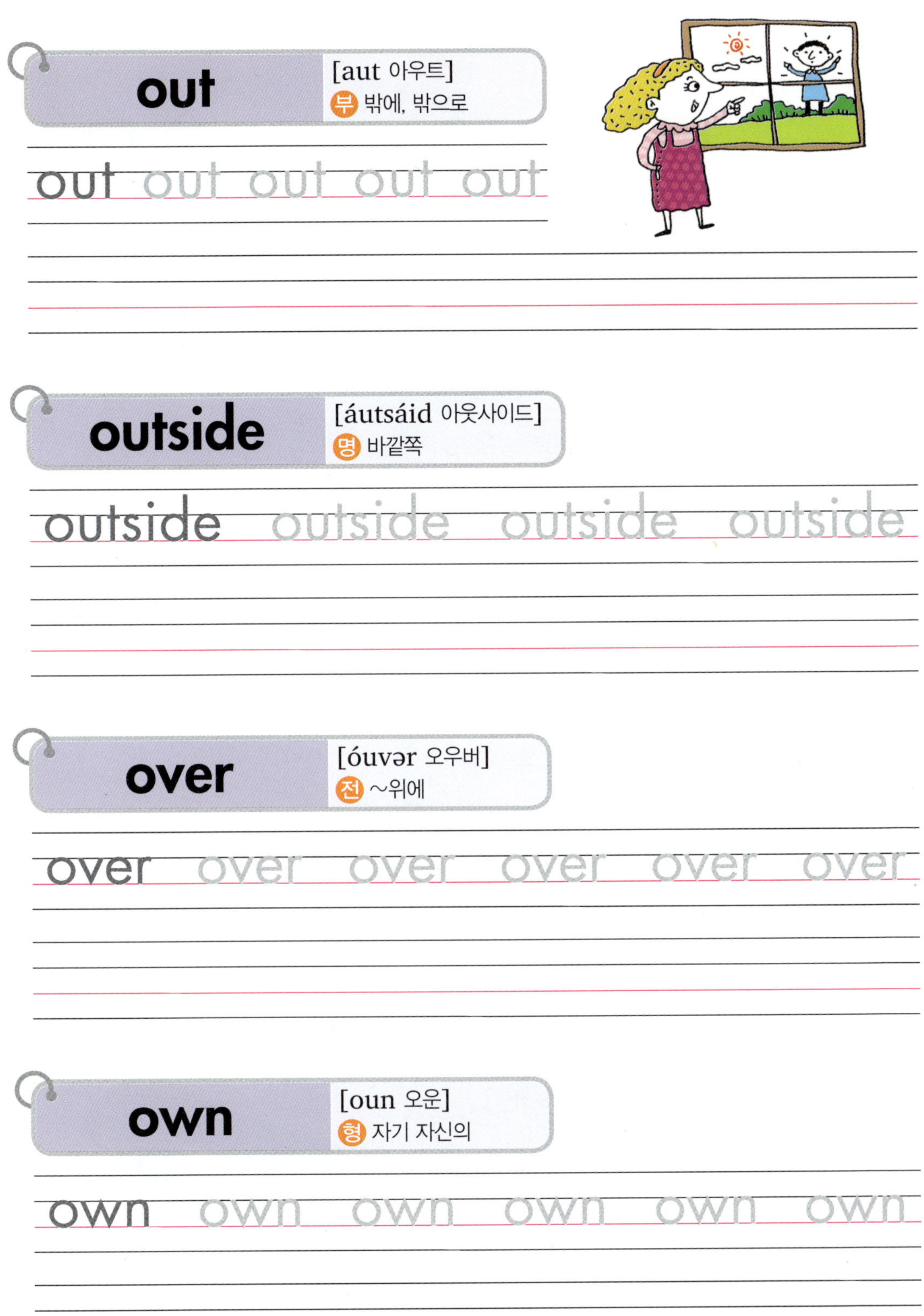

out

[aut 아우트]
부 밖에, 밖으로

out out out out out

outside

[áutsáid 아웃사이드]
명 바깥쪽

outside outside outside outside

over

[óuvər 오우버]
전 ~위에

over over over over over over

own

[oun 오운]
형 자기 자신의

own own own own own own

Pp

paint
[peint 페인트]
명 페인트, 그림물감

paint　paint　paint　paint　paint

palace
[pǽlis 팰리스]
명 궁전

palace　palace　palace　palace

pants
[pænts 팬츠]
명 바지

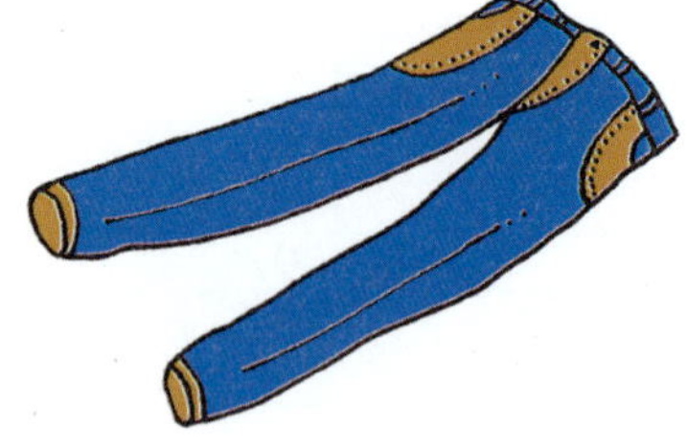

pants　pants　pants

192

paper

[péipər 페이퍼]
명 종이

paper　　paper

parent

[pέərənt 페어런트]
명 부모

parent　　parent　　parent　　parent

park

[pɑːrk 파-크]
명 공원

park　　park　　park

part

[pɑːrt 파-트]
명 일부, 부분

part　part　part　part　part　part

party

[pá:rti 파-티]
명 파티, 모임

party party party party party

pass

[pæs 패스]
동 지나가다, 합격하다

pass pass pass

past

[pæst 패스트]
명 과거

past past past past past past

path

[pæθ 패쓰]
명 (작은) 길

path path path

pay

[pei 페이]
동 지불하다

pay pay pay pay

peace

[piːs 피-스]
명 평화

peace peace peace peace peace

peanut

[píːnʌt 피-넛]
명 땅콩

peanut peanut peanut peanut

pen

[pen 펜]
명 펜

pen pen pen pen

pencil

[pénsəl 펜설]
명 연필

pencil pencil pencil

people

[píːpl 피-플]
명 사람들, 민족

people people people people

perfect

[pə́ːrfikt 퍼-픽트]
형 완전한

perfect perfect perfect perfect

perhaps

[pərhǽps 퍼햅스]
부 아마(도)

perhaps perhaps perhaps perhaps

person

[pə́:rsən 퍼-선]
명 사람

person　person　person　person

pet

[pet 펫]
명 애완동물

pet pet pet pet pet

phone

[foun 포운]
명 전화(기)

phone phone phone

piano

[piǽnou 피애노우]
명 피아노

piano piano piano piano piano

pick

[pik 픽]
동 따다, 골라잡다

pick pick pick pick pick pick

picnic

[píknik 피크닉]
명 소풍

picnic picnic picnic picnic picnic

picture

[píktʃər 픽춰]
명 그림

picture picture

piece

[piːs 피-스]
명 조각

piece piece piece piece piece

pig

[pig 피그]
명 돼지

pig pig pig pig pig pig pig

pillow

[pílou 필로우]
명 베개

pillow pillow pillow

pilot

[páilət 파일럿]
명 (비행기)조종사

pilot pilot pilot pilot pilot pilot

pin

[pin 핀]
명 핀, 못, 바늘

pin pin pin pin pin

pineapple

[páinæpl 파인애플]
명 파인애플

pineapple　pineapple　pineapple

pink

[piŋk 핑크]
명 연분홍색

pink　pink　pink　pink　pink　pink

place

[pleis 플레이스]
명 장소

place　place　place

plan

[plæn 플랜]
명 계획

plan　plan　plan

plane
[plein 플레인]
명 비행기

plane　plane　plane

plant
[plænt 플랜트]
명 식물

plant　plant　plant　plant　plant

play
[plei 플레이]
동 놀다, 연주하다

play　play　play

playground
[pleigràund 플레이그라운드]
명 운동장

playground　playground playground

player
[pléiər 플레이어]
명 선수

player player player

please
[pli:z 플리-즈]
부 제발, 부디

please please please please

plenty
[plénti 플렌티]
형 많은, 충분한

plenty plenty plenty plenty plenty

pocket
[pákit 파킷]
명 호주머니

pocket pocket

poem

[póuim 포우임]
명 시

poem poem poem poem poem

point

[pɔint 포인트]
명 요점, 목적

point point point point point

police

[pəlíːs 펄리-스]
명 경찰

police police police

pool

[puːl 푸-울]
명 수영장, 물웅덩이

pool pool pool pool

poor
[puər 푸어]
형 가난한

poor poor poor

post-office
[póust-ɔ̀(:)fis 포우스트–오피스]
명 우체국

post-office post-office post-office

potato
[pətéitou 퍼테이토우]
명 감자

potato potato potato potato

power
[páuər 파우어]
명 힘

power power power

practice practice practice practice

prepare prepare

present present

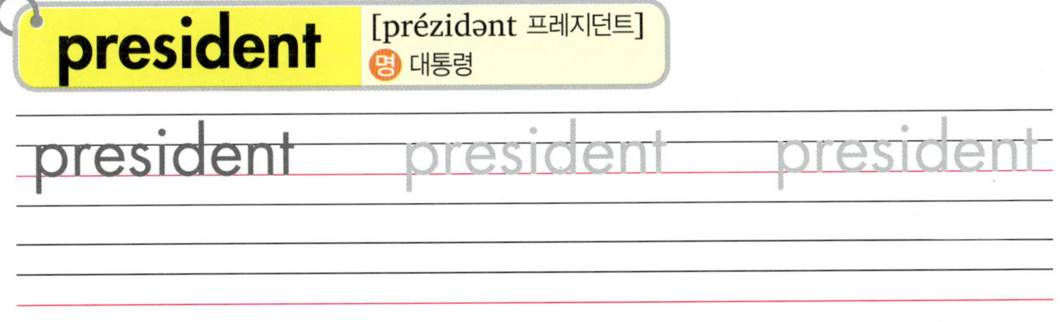

president president president

pretty

[príti 프리티]
형 예쁜, 귀여운

pretty   pretty   pretty   pretty   pretty

price

[prais 프라이스]
명 가격

price   price   price

prince

[prins 프린스]
명 왕자

prince   prince   prince   prince   prince

princess

[prínsis 프린시스]
명 공주, 왕비

princess   princess   princess   princess

prize
[praiz 프라이즈]
명 상

prize　prize　prize

problem
[prábləm 프라블럼]
명 문제

problem problem problem problem

promise
[prámis 프라미스]
명 약속

promise　promise

proud
[praud 프라우드]
형 자랑으로 여기는

proud proud proud proud proud

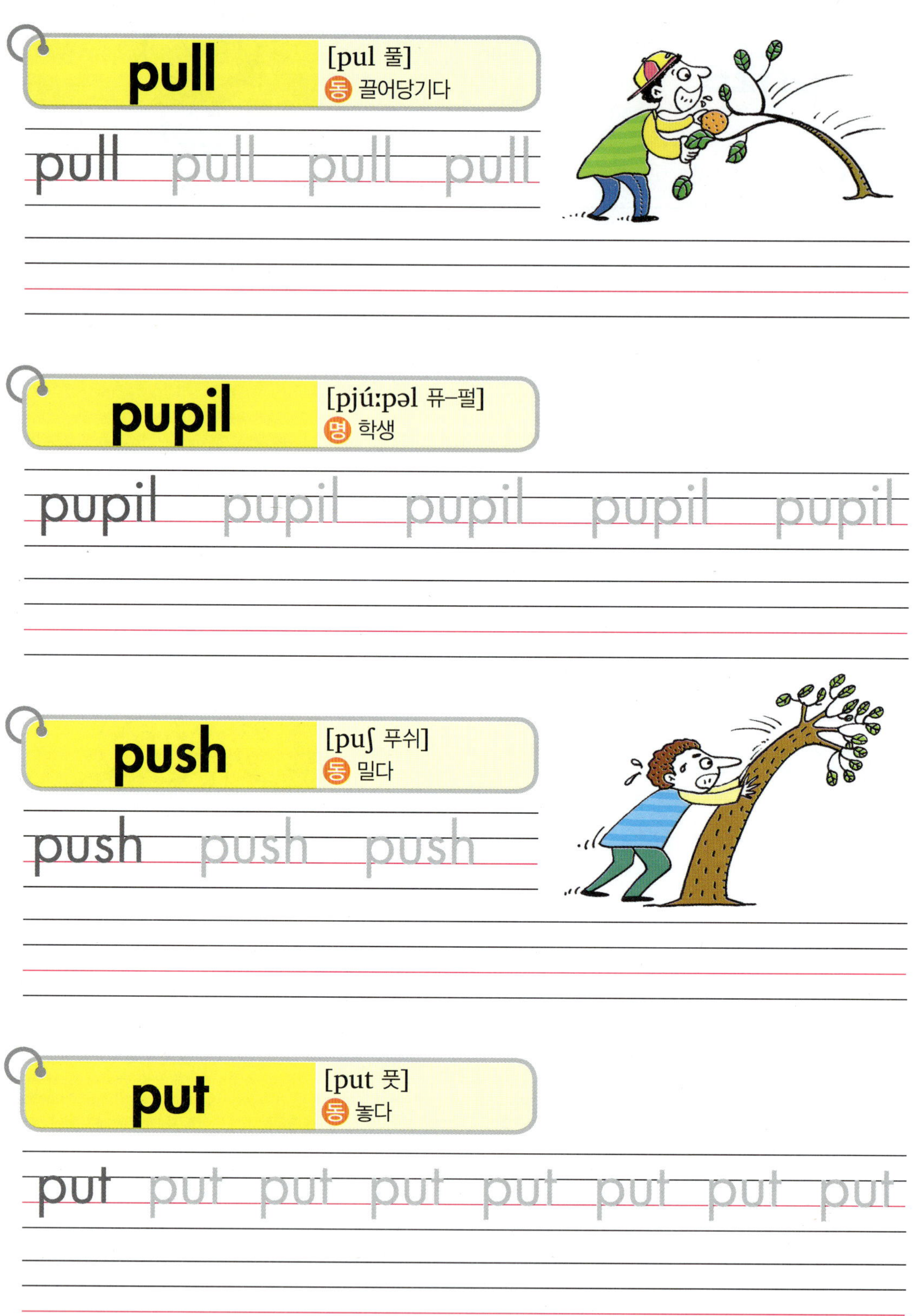

pull
[pul 풀]
동 끌어당기다

pull　pull　pull　pull

pupil
[pjúːpəl 퓨–펄]
명 학생

pupil　pupil　pupil　pupil　pupil

push
[puʃ 푸쉬]
동 밀다

push　push　push

put
[put 풋]
동 놓다

put　put　put　put　put　put　put　put

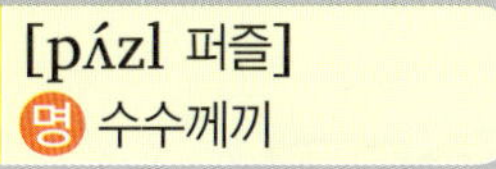

puzzle   puzzle   puzzle   puzzle

Qq

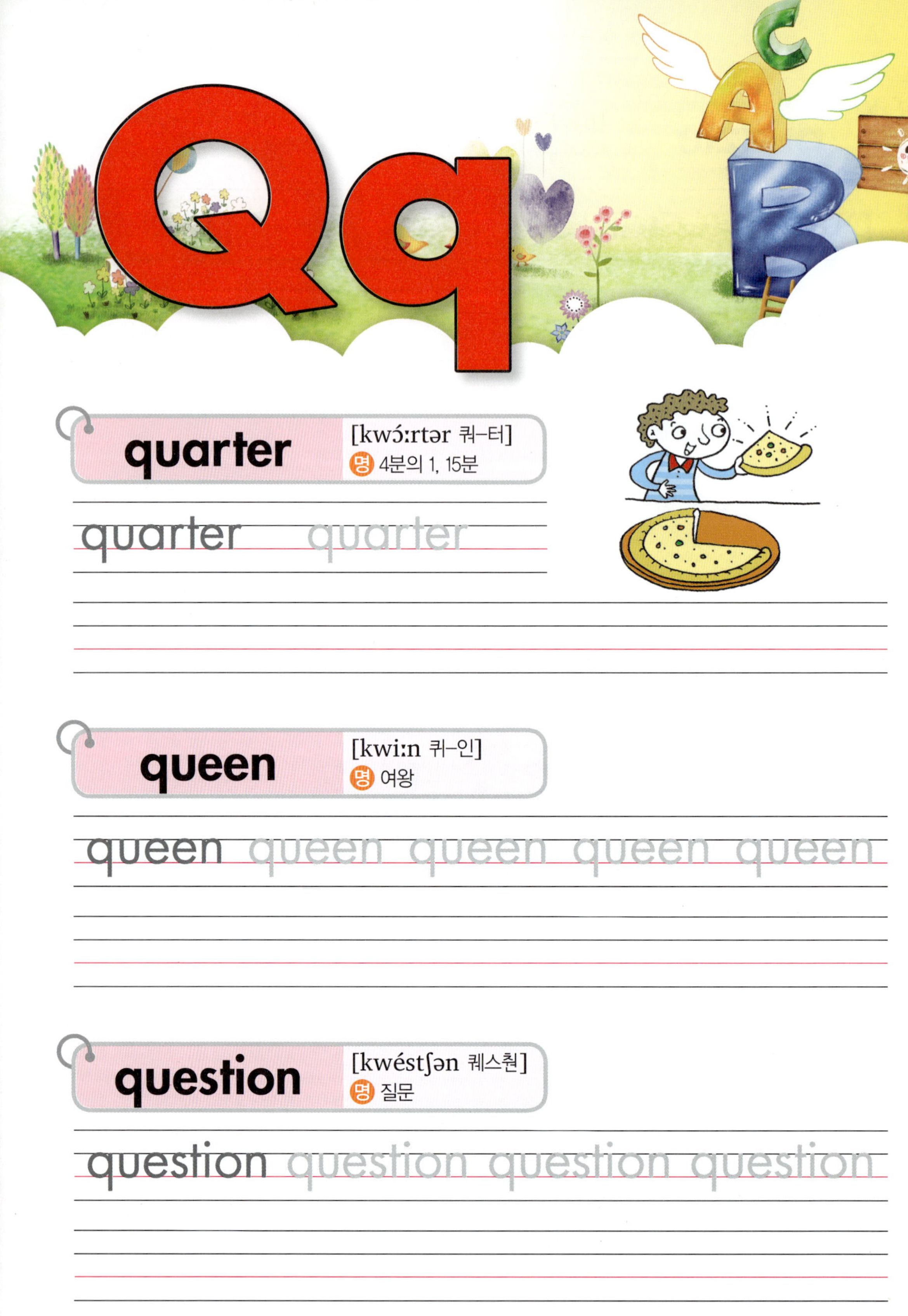

quarter
[kwɔ́:rtər 쿼-터]
명 4분의 1, 15분

quarter　quarter

queen
[kwi:n 퀴-인]
명 여왕

queen　queen　queen　queen　queen

question
[kwéstʃən 퀘스쳔]
명 질문

question　question　question　question

quick

[kwik 퀵]
형 빠른

quick　quick　quick　quick　quick

quickly

[kwíkli 퀴클리]
부 빠르게

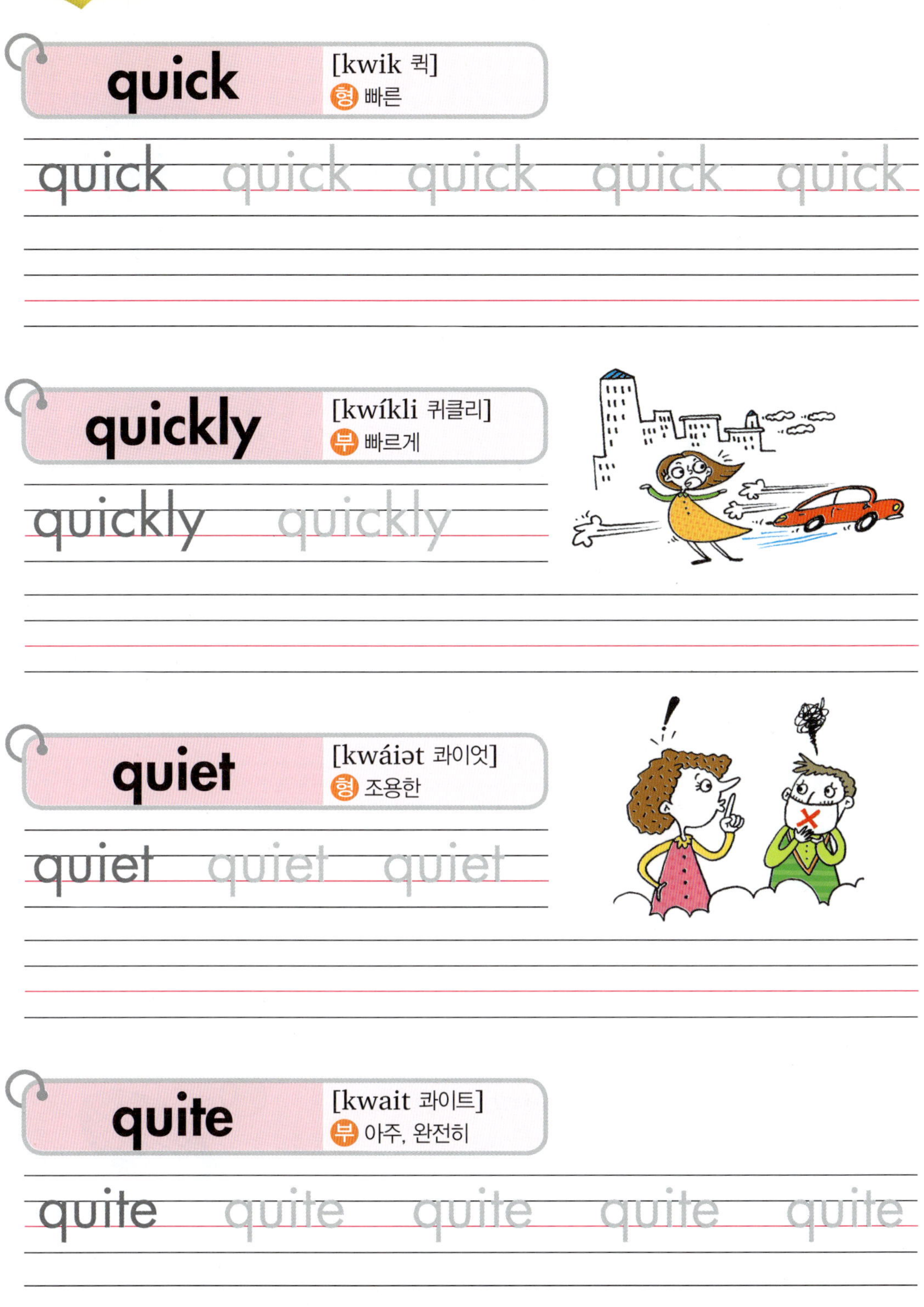

quickly　quickly

quiet

[kwáiət 콰이엇]
형 조용한

quiet　quiet　quiet

quite

[kwait 콰이트]
부 아주, 완전히

quite　quite　quite　quite　quite

Rr

rabbit
[rǽbit 래빗]
명 토끼

rabbit rabbit rabbit

race
[reis 레이스]
명 경주

race race race race race race

racket
[rǽkit 래킷]
명 라켓, 채

racket racket racket

radio
[réidiòu 레이디오우]
명 라디오

radio　radio　radio

railroad
[réilròud 레일로우드]
명 철도

railroad　railroad　railroad　railroad

rain
[rein 레인]
명 비

rain　rain　rain　rain

rainbow
[réinbòu 레인보우]
명 무지개

rainbow　rainbow　rainbow　rainbow

rainy

[réini 레이니]
형 비오는

rainy　rainy　rainy　rainy　rainy

ran

[ræn 랜]
동 run(달리다)의 과거(달렸다)

ran　ran　ran　ran　ran

reach

[ri:tʃ 리-취]
동 도착하다

reach　reach　reach　reach　reach

read

[ri:d 리-드]
동 읽다

read　read　read

ready

[rédi 레디]
형 준비가 된

ready　ready　ready　ready　ready

real

[ríːəl 리-얼]
형 진짜의

real　real　real　real　real　real　real

really

[ríːəli 리-얼리]
부 정말로

really　really　really

reason

[ríːzən 리-전]
명 이유

reason　reason　reason　reason

record

[rékə:rd 레커-드]
명 기록

record　record

red

[red 레드]
형 빨간

red red red red red red red red

remember

[rimémbə:r 리멤버-]
동 기억하다

remember remember

repeat

[ripí:t 리피-트]
동 되풀이하다, 반복하다

repeat repeat repeat repeat

report

[ripɔ́:rt 리포-트]
동 보고하다

report report report report report

rest

[rest 레스트]
명 휴식

rest rest rest rest

return

[ritə́:rn 리터-언]
동 되돌아가다

return return return

ribbon

[ríbən 리번]
명 리본, 띠

ribbon ribbon ribbon ribbon

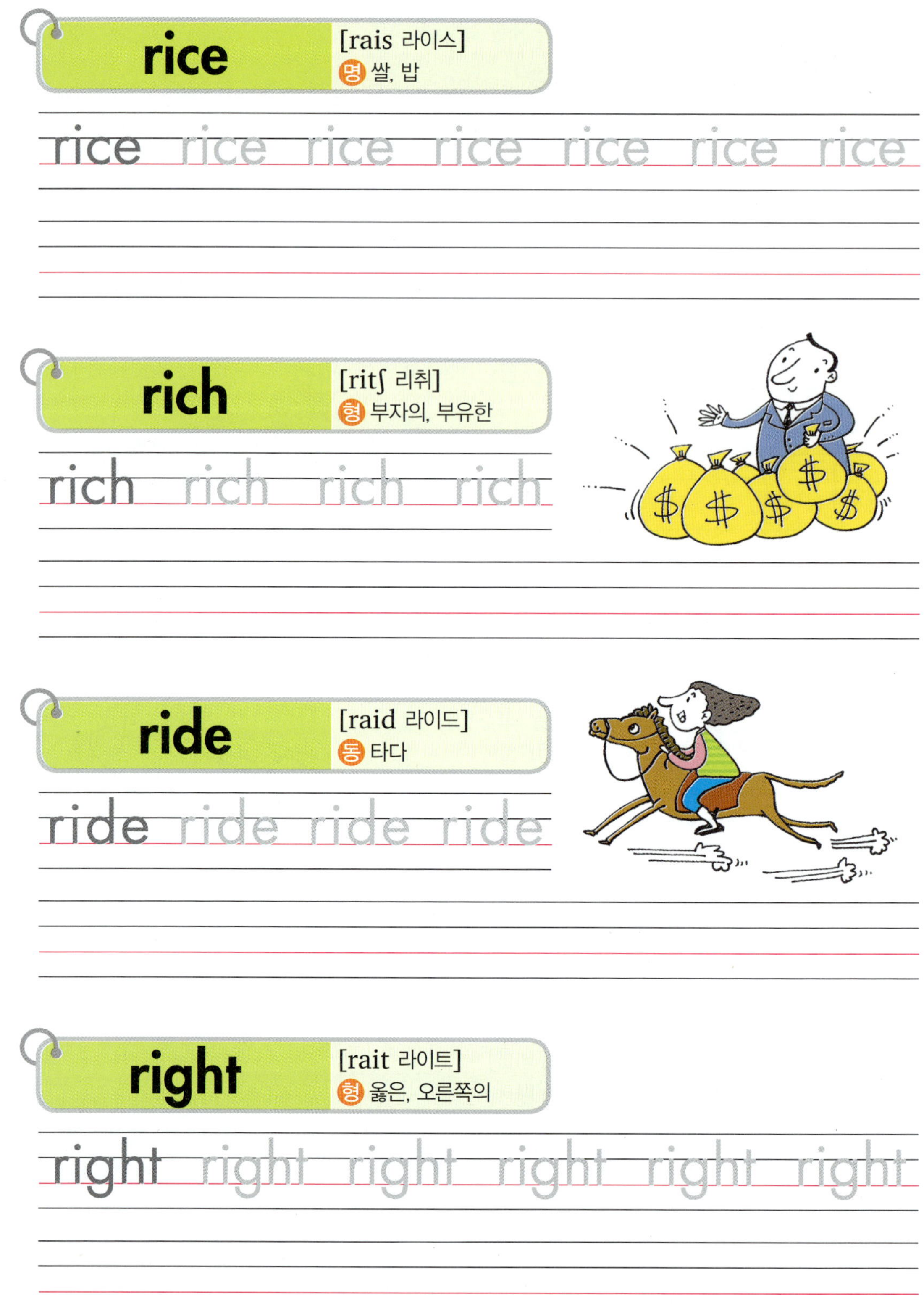

rice
[rais 라이스]
명 쌀, 밥

rice rice rice rice rice rice rice

rich
[ritʃ 리취]
형 부자의, 부유한

rich rich rich rich

ride
[raid 라이드]
동 타다

ride ride ride ride

right
[rait 라이트]
형 옳은, 오른쪽의

right right right right right right

ring

[riŋ 링]
명 고리, 반지

ring   ring   ring   ring

rise

[raiz 라이즈]
동 일어나다, (해, 달)떠오르다

rise   rise   rise   rise   rise   rise   rise

river

[rívəːr 리버–]
명 강

river   river   river   river   river   river

road

[roud 로우드]
명 길, 도로

road   road   road

robot

[róubət 로우벗]
명 로봇

robot　robot　robot

rock

[rɑk 락]
명 바위

rock　rock　rock　rock　rock　rock

rocket

[rɑ́kit 라킷]
명 로켓

rocket　rocket　rocket　rocket　rocket

roll

[roul 로울]
동 구르다

roll　roll　roll　roll

roof
[ru:f 루-프]
명 지붕

roof roof roof roof

room
[ru:m 루-움]
명 방

room room room room room

rope
[roup 로우프]
명 밧줄

rope rope rope

rose
[rouz 로우즈]
명 장미

rose rose rose rose rose rose

round

[raund 라운드]
형 둥근

round　round　round　round　round

ruler

[rú:lə:r 루-울러-]
명 자

ruler　ruler　ruler

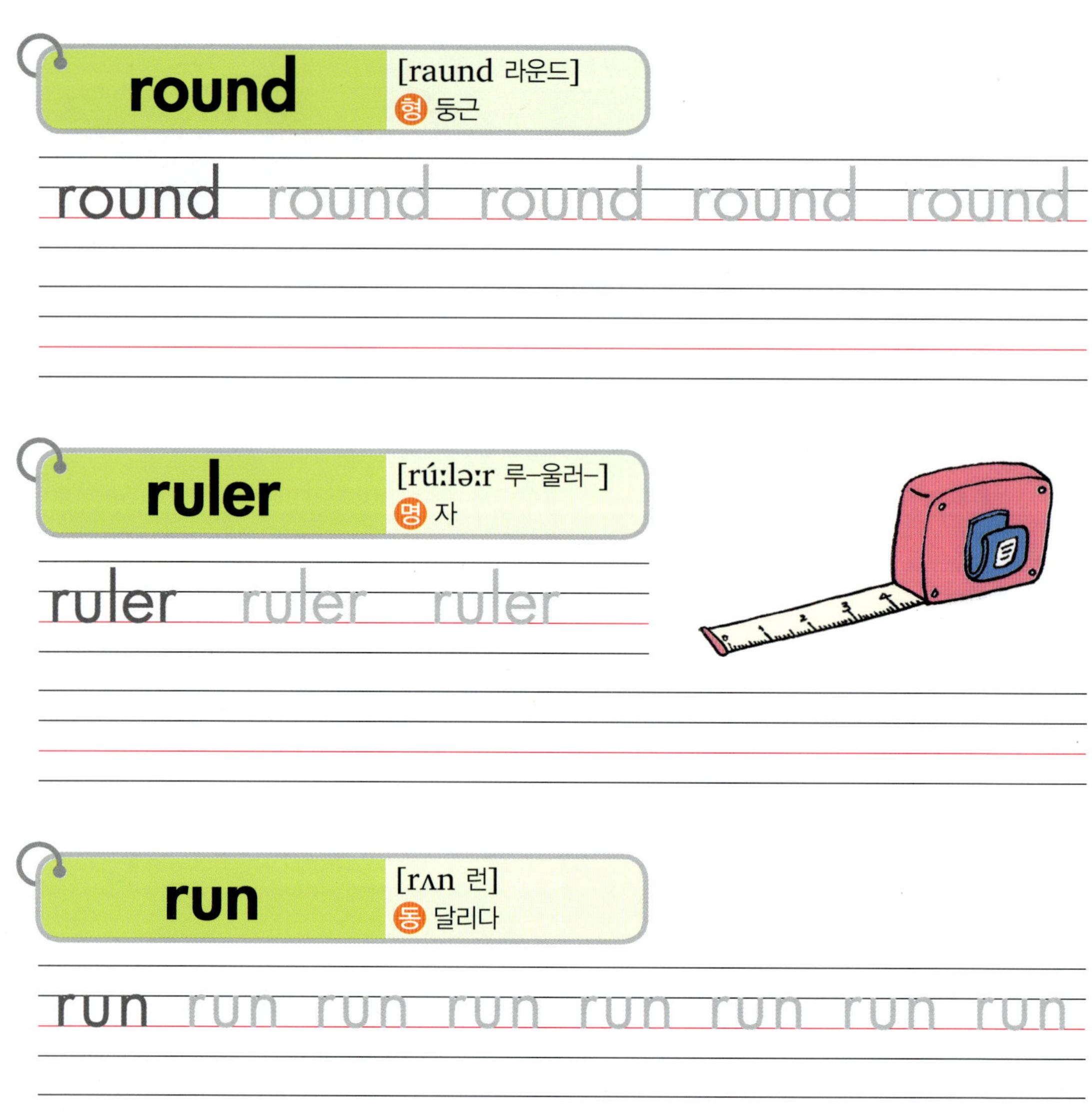

run

[rʌn 런]
동 달리다

run　run　run　run　run　run　run　run

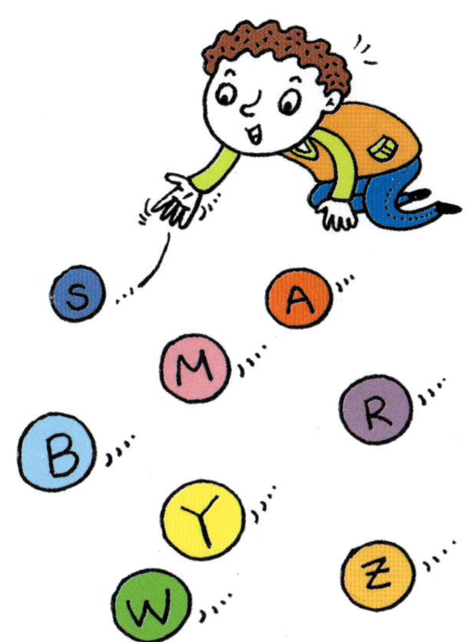

S
A
M
R
B
Y
W
Z

Ss

sad
[sæd 샛]
형 슬픈

sad　sad　sad　sad

safe
[seif 세이프]
형 안전한

safe　safe　safe　safe　safe　safe

sail
[seil 세일]
동 항해하다

sail　sail　sail　sail　sail　sail　sail

salt

[sɔːlt 소-올트]
명 소금

salt salt salt salt salt salt salt

same

[seim 세임]
형 같은

same same same

sand

[sænd 샌드]
명 모래

sand sand sand sand sand

sandwich

[sǽndwitʃ 샌드위취]
명 샌드위치

sandwich sandwich

Santa Claus
[sǽntəklɔ̀s 샌터클로스]
명 산타클로스

Sánta Clàus   Sánta Clàus

Saturday
[sǽtə:rdi 새터–디]
명 토요일

Saturday   Saturday   Saturday

save
[seiv 세이브]
동 구하다, 저축하다

save   save   save

say
[sei 세이]
동 말하다

say   say   say   say

school

[sku:l 스쿠-울]
명 학교

school　school　school　school

sea

[si: 시-]
명 바다

sea　sea　sea　sea

season

[síːzən 시-전]
명 계절

season　season　season　season

seat

[si:t 시-트]
명 자리, 자석

seat　seat　seat　seat　seat　seat　seat

second

[sék-ənd 세커-언드]
형 제2의, 둘째 번의

second   second   second   second

secret

[síːkrit 시-크릿]
명 비밀

secret   secret   secret

see

[siː 시-]
동 보다

see   see   see   see

seesaw

[síːsɔ̀ː 시-소-]
명 시소(놀이)

seesaw   seesaw   seesaw   seesaw

sell

[sel 셀]
동 팔다

sell　sell　sell　sell　sell

send

[send 센드]
동 보내다

send　send　send

sentence

[séntəns 센턴스]
명 문장

sentence　sentence　sentence

September

[səptémbər 섭템버]
명 9월

September　September　September

service
[sə́:rvis 서-비스]
몡 봉사

service　service　service　service

seven
[sévn 세븐]
몡 7, 일곱

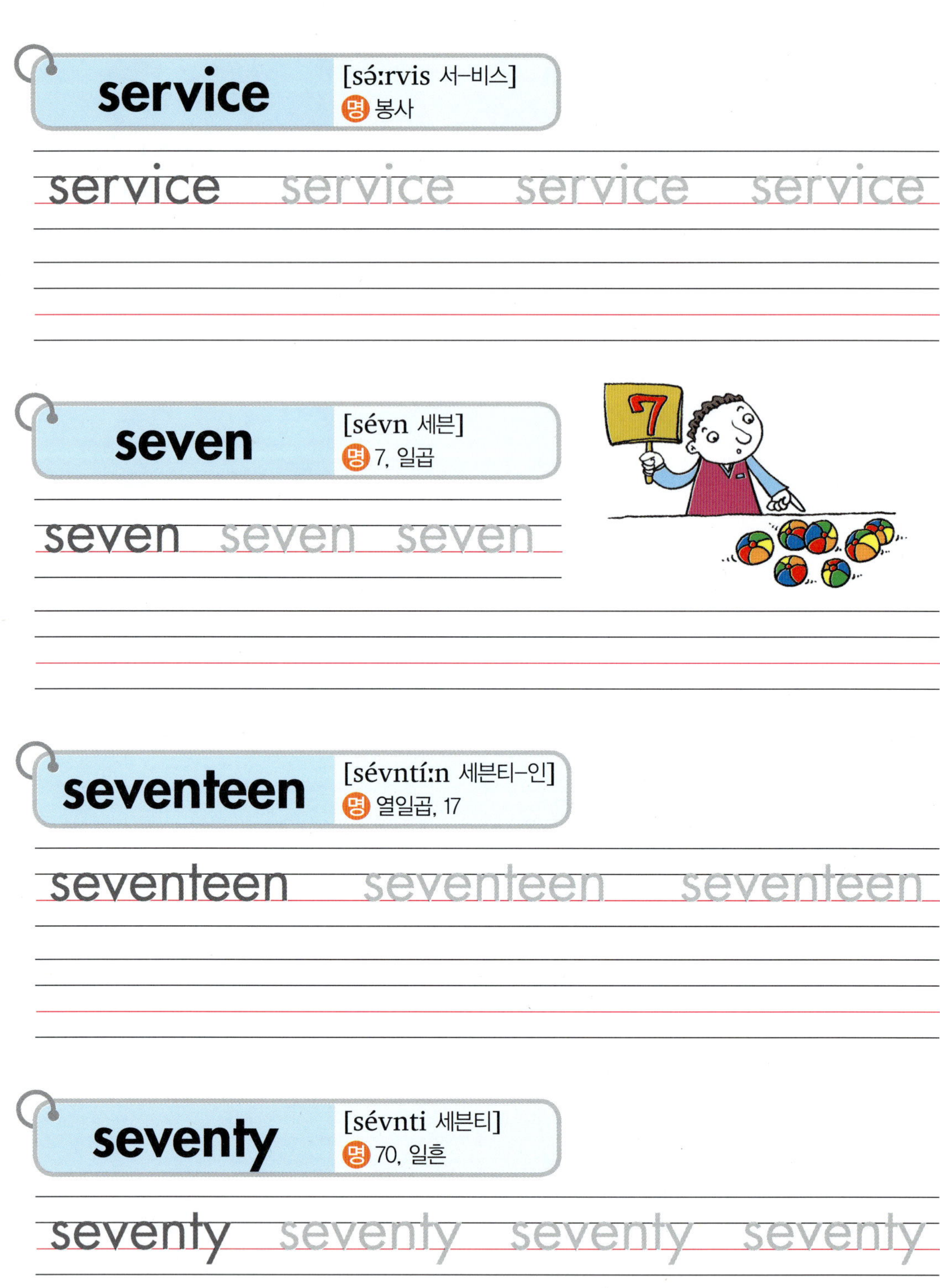

seven　seven　seven

seventeen
[sévntí:n 세븐티-인]
몡 열일곱, 17

seventeen　seventeen　seventeen

seventy
[sévnti 세븐티]
몡 70, 일흔

seventy　seventy　seventy　seventy

shall

[ʃæl 쉘]
조 ～일(할) 것이다

shall　shall　shall　shall　shall　shall

shape

[ʃeip 쉐이프]
명 모양

shape　shape　shape

sheep

[ʃiːp 쉬-입]
명 양

sheep　sheep　sheep　sheep　sheep

shine

[ʃain 샤인]
동 빛나다, 빛나게 하다

shine　shine　shine

ship

[ʃip 쉽]
명 배

ship　ship　ship　ship　ship　ship

shirt

[ʃəːrt 셔-트]
명 셔츠

shirt　shirt　shirt　shirt　shirt　shirt

shoe

[ʃuː 슈-]
명 신, 구두

shoe　shoe　shoe　shoe　shoe　shoe

shoot

[ʃuːt 슈-트]
동 쏘다

shoot　shoot　shoot

shop [ʃap 샵]
명 가게, 상점

shop shop shop

shopping [ʃápiŋ 샤핑]
명 쇼핑

shopping shopping shopping

short [ʃɔːrt 쇼-트]
형 짧은

short short short

should [ʃud 슈드]
조 ~해야 한다

should should should should

shoulder

[ʃóuldəːr 쇼울더-]
명 어깨

shoulder   shoulder   shoulder

shout

[ʃaut 샤우트]
동 외치다

shout   shout   shout

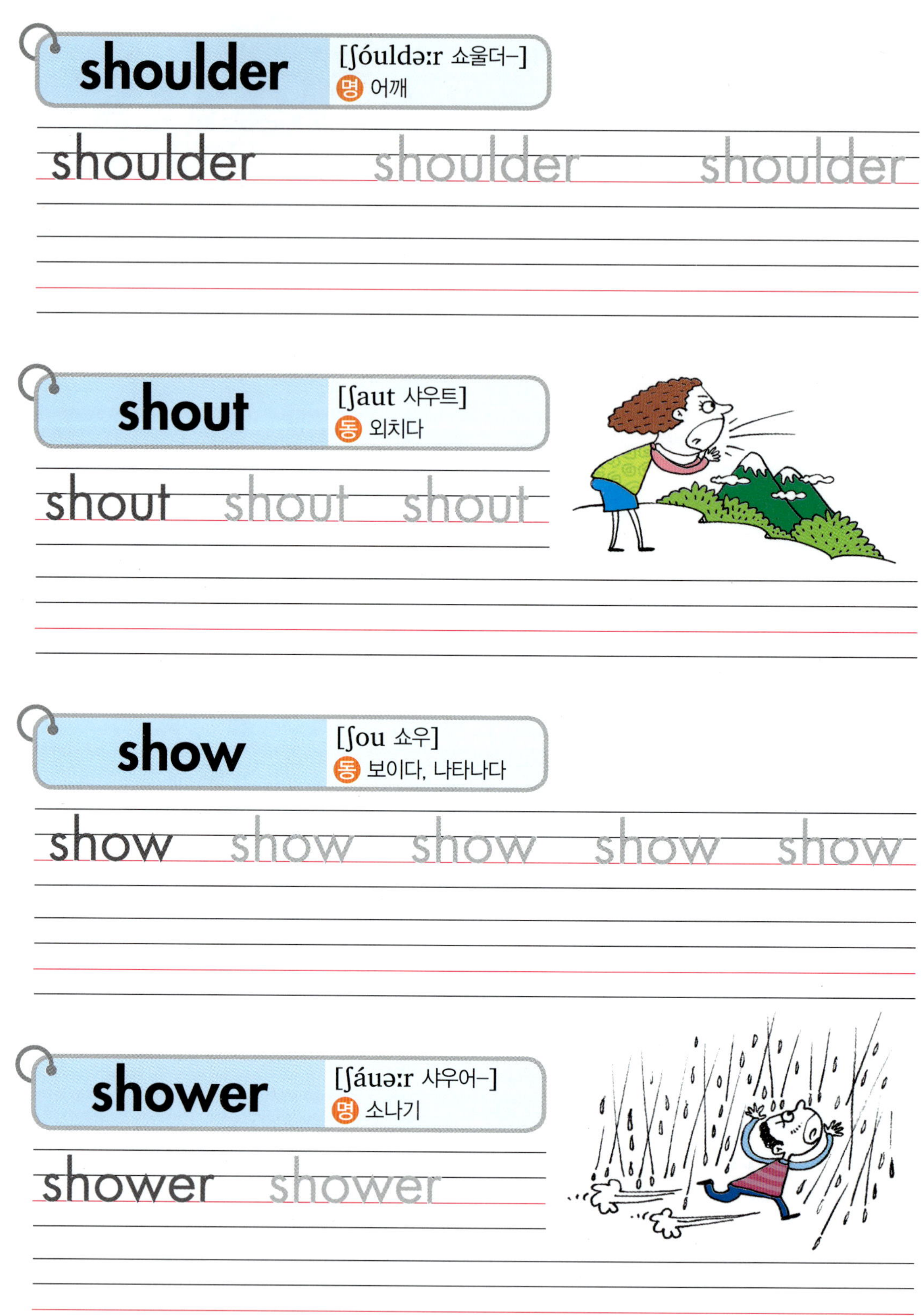

show

[ʃou 쇼우]
동 보이다, 나타나다

show   show   show   show   show

shower

[ʃáuəːr 샤우어-]
명 소나기

shower   shower

shut
[ʃʌt 셧]
(동) 닫다

shut shut shut shut shut shut shut

sick
[sik 식]
(형) 아픈, 병에 걸린

sick sick sick sick

side
[said 사이드]
(명) 쪽, 옆

side side side side side side

sign
[sain 사인]
(동) 사인(서명)하다

sign sign sign

silver

[sílvəːr 실버–]
명 은

silver　silver　silver　silver　silver

sing

[siŋ 싱]
동 노래하다

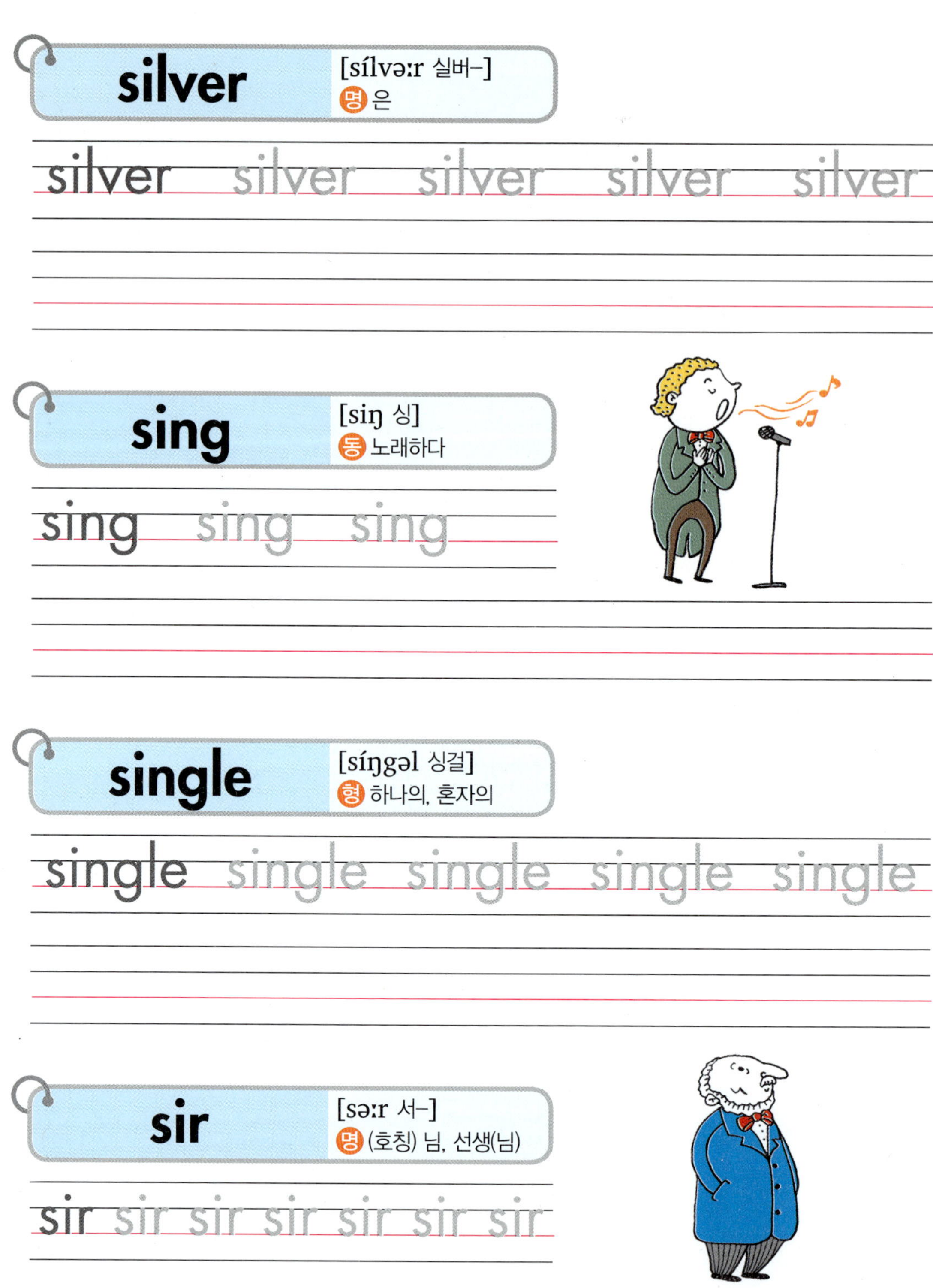

sing　sing　sing

single

[síŋgəl 싱걸]
형 하나의, 혼자의

single　single　single　single　single

sir

[səːr 서–]
명 (호칭) 님, 선생(님)

sir sir sir sir sir sir sir

sister

[sístəːr 시스터-]
명 여자 형제

sister　sister　sister

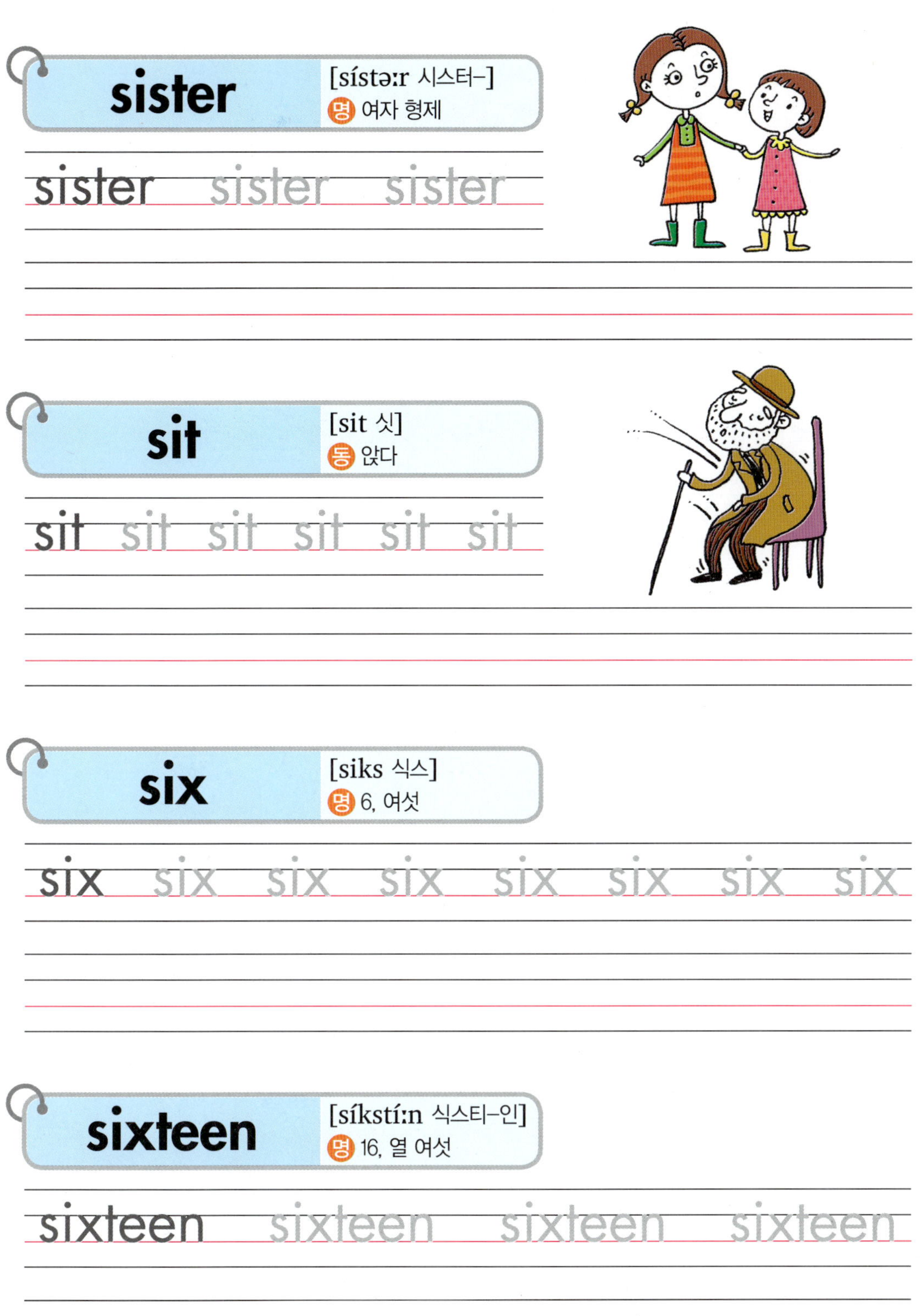

sit

[sit 싯]
동 앉다

sit sit sit sit sit sit

six

[siks 식스]
명 6, 여섯

six six six six six six six six

sixteen

[síkstíːn 식스티-인]
명 16, 열 여섯

sixteen sixteen sixteen sixteen

sixty

[síksti 식스티]
명 60, 예순

sixty　sixty　sixty　sixty　sixty　sixty

size

[saiz 사이즈]
명 크기

size　size　size　size　size　size

skate

[skeit 스케이트]
명 스케이트

skate　skate　skate

ski

[ski: 스키-]
명 스키

ski　ski　ski　ski　ski

skirt

[skəːrt 스커-트]
명 치마

skirt   skirt   skirt   skirt

sky

[skai 스카이]
명 하늘

sky   sky   sky   sky   sky   sky   sky   sky

sleep

[sliːp 슬리-입]
동 잠자다

sleep   sleep   sleep   sleep   sleep

sleepy

[slíːpi 슬리-피]
형 졸린

sleepy   sleepy   sleepy

slow
[slou 슬로우]
형 느린

slow　　slow　　slow

slowly
[slóuli 슬로울리]
부 천천히, 느리게

slowly　　slowly　　slowly　　slowly

small
[smɔːl 스모―올]
형 작은

small　　small　　small

smart
[smɑːrt 스마―트]
형 똑똑한

smart　　smart　　smart　　smart　　smart

smell

[smel 스멜]
명 냄새

smell　smell　smell　smell　smell

smile

[smail 스마일]
동 미소짓다

smile　smile　smile

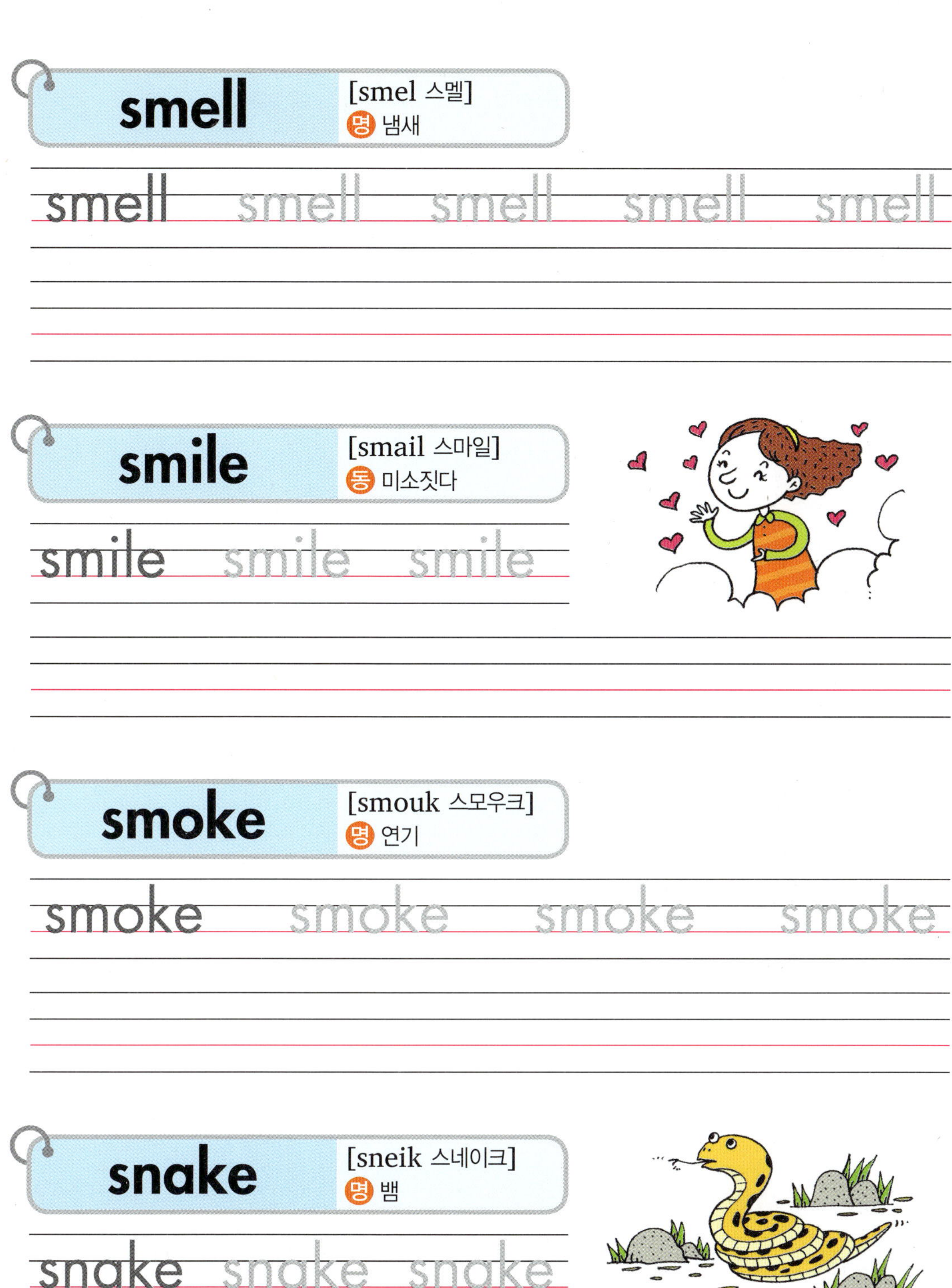

smoke

[smouk 스모우크]
명 연기

smoke　smoke　smoke　smoke

snake

[sneik 스네이크]
명 뱀

snake　snake　snake

snow

[snou 스노우]
명 눈

snow　snow　snow

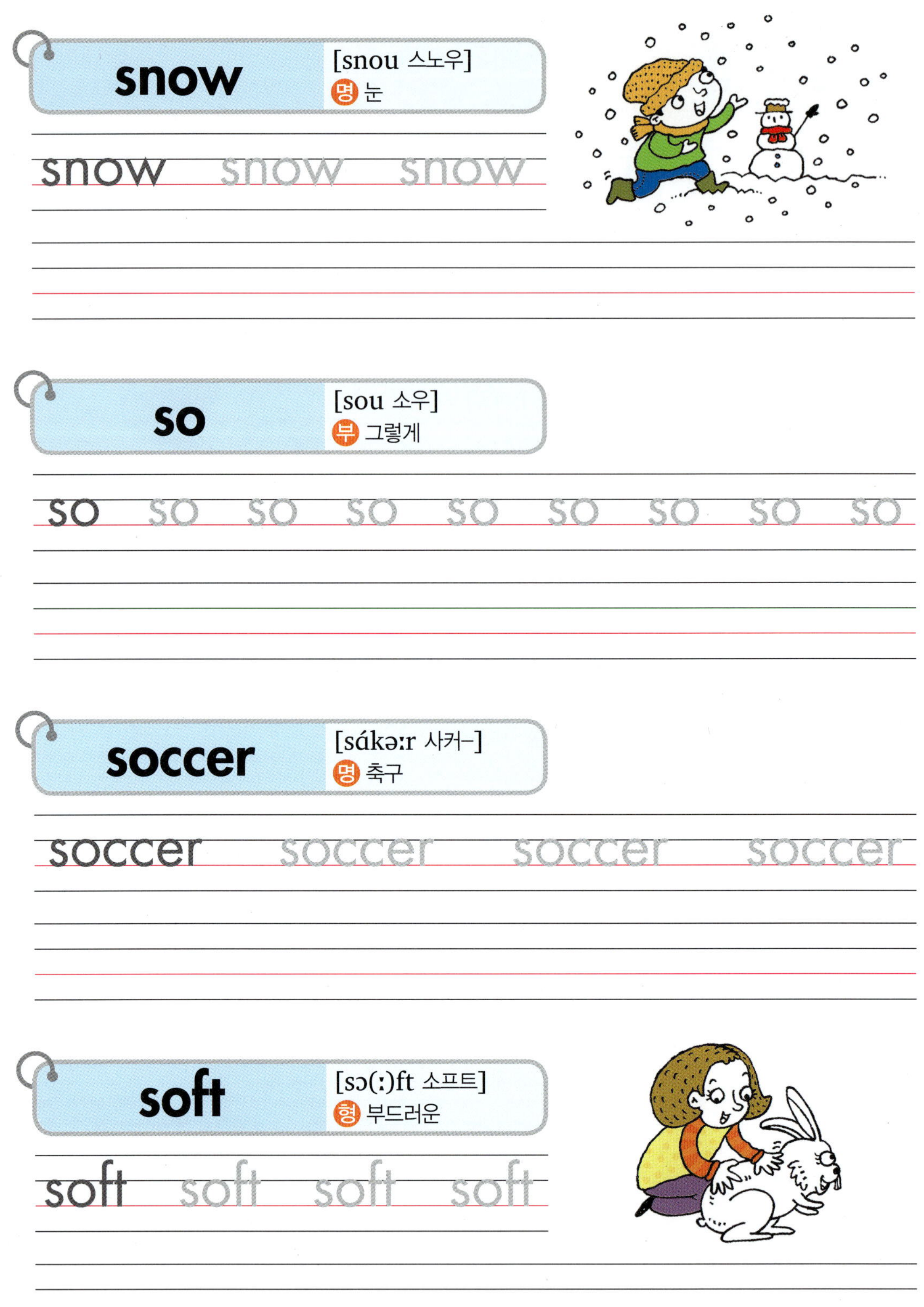

so

[sou 소우]
부 그렇게

so　so　so　so　so　so　so　so　so　so

soccer

[sάkə:r 사커-]
명 축구

soccer　soccer　soccer　soccer

soft

[sɔ(ː)ft 소프트]
형 부드러운

soft　soft　soft　soft

soldier

[sóuldʒəːr 소울줘-]
명 군인

soldier　soldier　soldier　soldier

some

[sʌm 섬]
형 약간의, 어떤

some　some　some　some　some

someone

[sʌ́mwʌ̀n 섬원]
대 누군가, 어떤 사람

someone　someone

something

[sʌ́mθiŋ 섬씽]
대 어떤 것, 무언가

something　something　something

son

[sʌn 선]
명 아들

son　son　son　son　son　son　son

song

[sɔ(ː)ŋ 송]
명 노래

song　song　song

soon

[suːn 수-운]
부 이윽고, 곧

soon　soon　soon　soon　soon　soon

sorry

[sɔ́ːri 소-리]
형 미안한, 유감스러운

sorry　sorry　sorry

sound

[saund 사운드]
명 소리, 음

sound sound sound

south

[sauθ 사우쓰]
명 남쪽

south south south south south

speak

[spi:k 스피-크]
동 말하다

speak speak speak

special

[spéʃ-əl 스페셜]
형 특별한

special special special special

speed

[spi:d 스피-드]
명 속도

speed   speed   speed   speed   speed

spell

[spel 스펠]
동 ~의 철자를 말하다

spell   spell   spell

spend

[spend 스펜드]
동 (돈)쓰다

spend   spend   spend   spend   spend

spoon

[spu:n 스푸-운]
명 숟가락

spoon   spoon   spoon

sport

[spɔːrt 스포-트]
명 스포츠, 운동

sport   sport   sport   sport   sport

spring

[spriŋ 스프링]
명 봄

spring   spring   spring

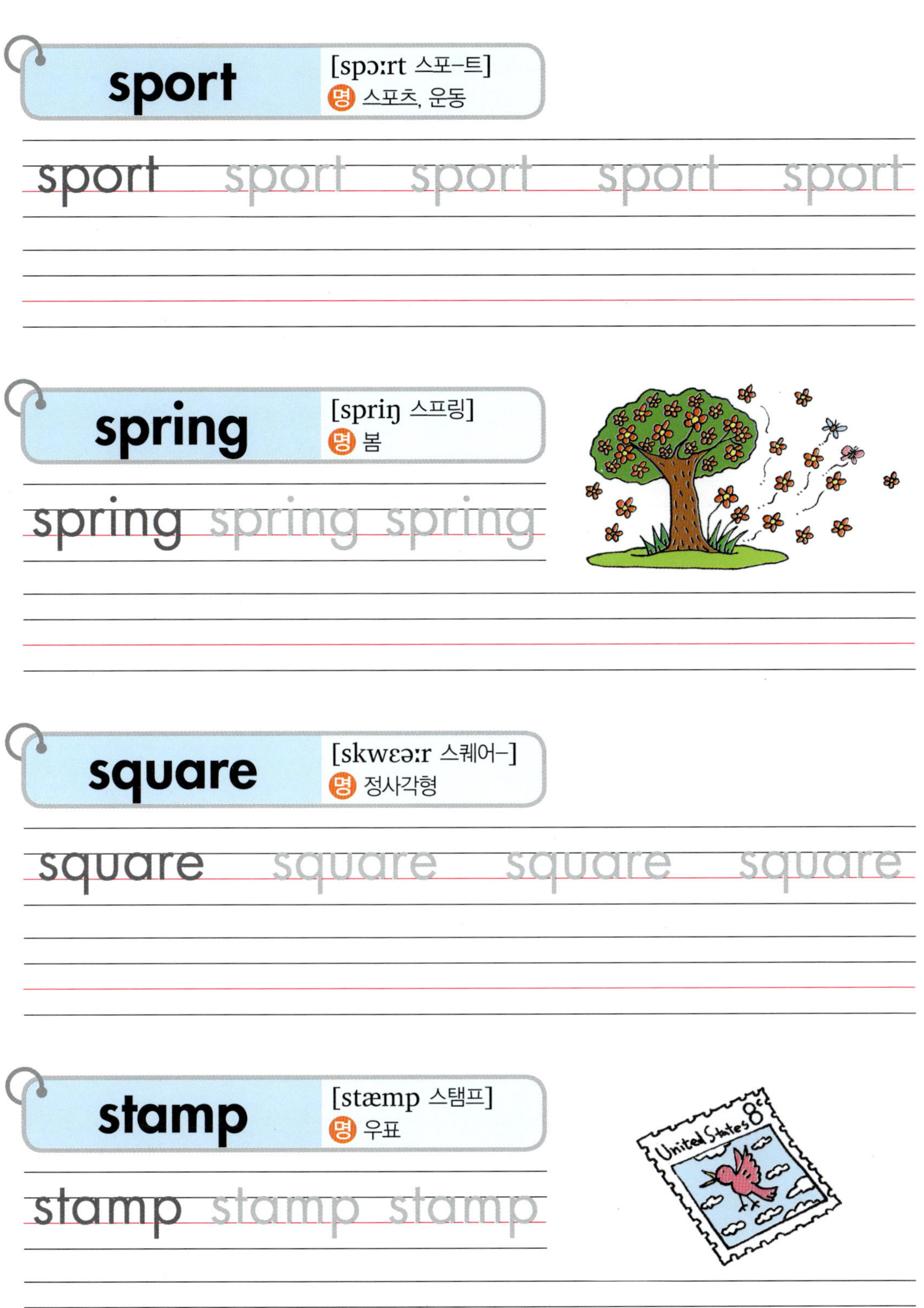

square

[skwɛəːr 스퀘어-]
명 정사각형

square   square   square   square

stamp

[stæmp 스탬프]
명 우표

stamp   stamp   stamp

stand

[stænd 스탠드]
동 (일어)서다

stand　stand　stand

star

[staːr 스타-]
명 별

star　star　star　star

start

[staːrt 스타-트]
동 출발하다

start　start　start　start　start　start

station

[stéiʃ-ən 스테이션]
명 역, 정거장

station　station　station　station

stay

[stei 스테이]
동 머무르다

stay　stay　stay　stay

step

[step 스텝]
명 걸음, 계단

step　step　step　step　step　step

stick

[stik 스틱]
명 막대기

stick stick stick stick

still

[stil 스틸]
부 아직(도), 여전히

still still still still still still still still

stocking

[stákiŋ 스타킹]
명 스타킹, 긴 양말

stone

[stoun 스토운]
명 돌

stop

[stɑp 스탑]
동 멈추다

store

[stɔːr 스토–]
명 가게

storm

[stɔːrm 스토–옴]
명 폭풍(우)

storm storm storm storm storm

story

[stɔ́ːri 스토–리]
명 이야기

story story story story story

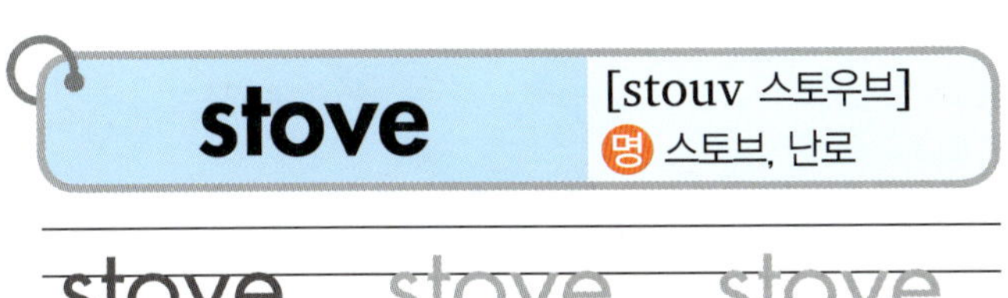

stove

[stouv 스토우브]
명 스토브, 난로

stove stove stove

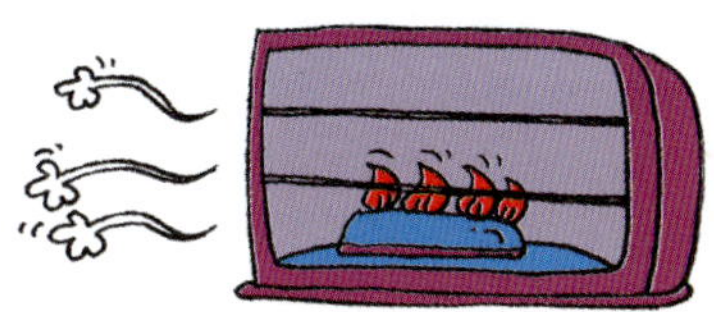

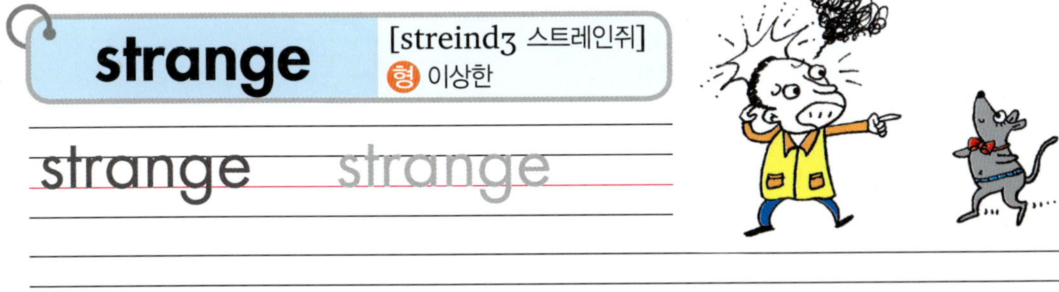

strange

[streindʒ 스트레인쥐]
형 이상한

strange strange

strawberry

[strɔ́:bèri 스트로-베리]
명 딸기

strawberry　strawberry　strawberry

street

[stri:t 스트리-트]
명 거리

street　street　street　street　street

strike

[straik 스트라이크]
동 치다, 때리다

strike　strike　strike

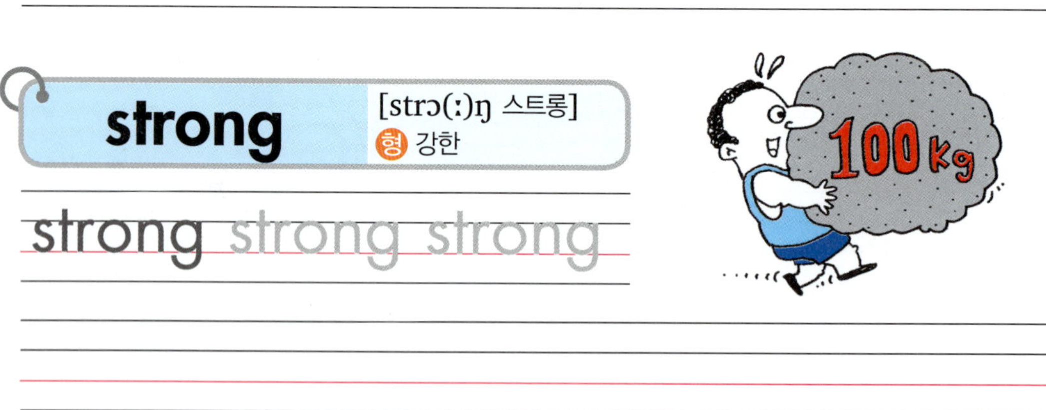

strong

[strɔ(:)ŋ 스트롱]
형 강한

strong strong strong

student

[stjúːd-ənt 스튜–던트]
명 학생

student   student   student   student

study

[stʌ́di 스터디]
동 공부하다

study   study   study

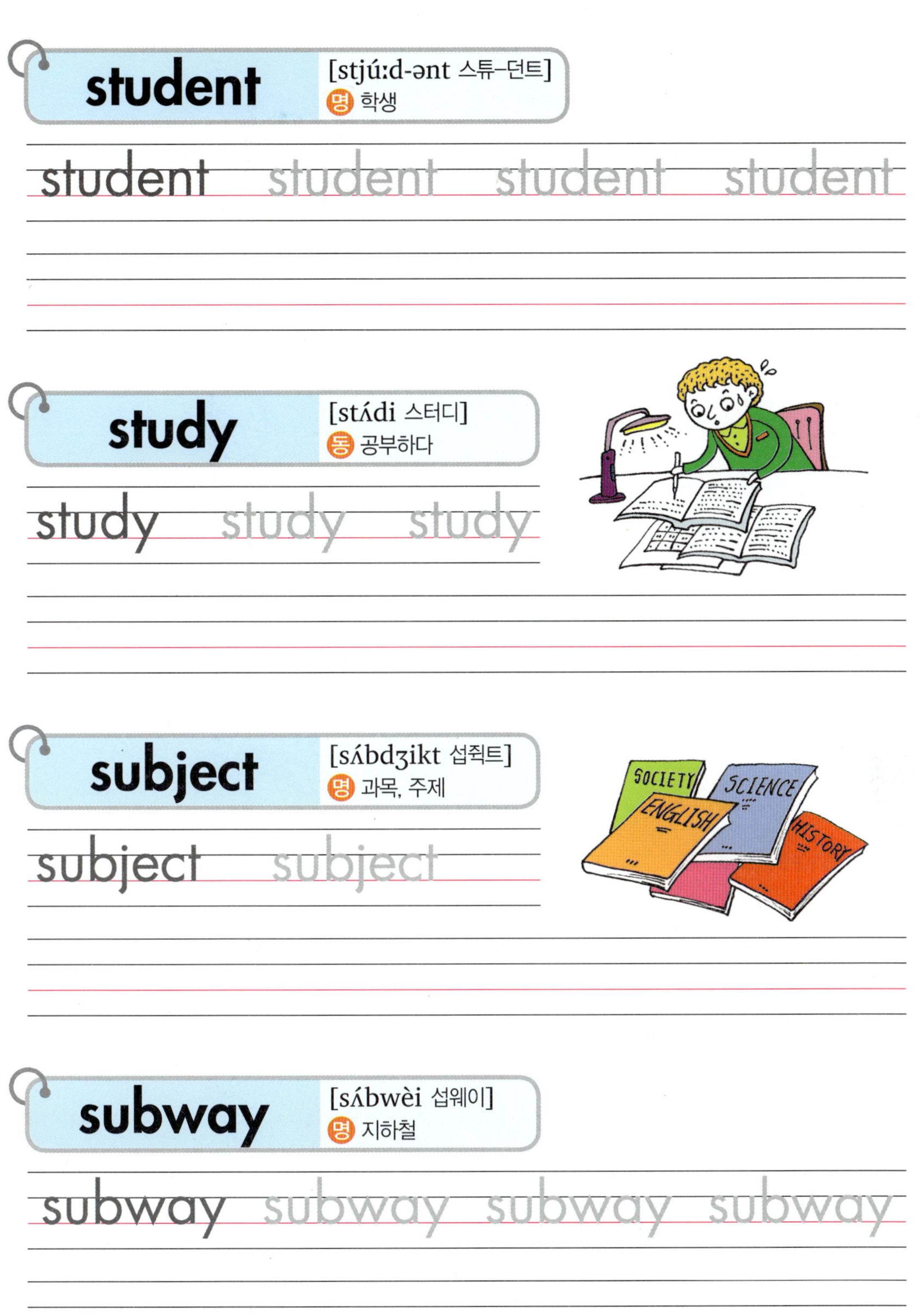

subject

[sʌ́bdʒikt 섭줵트]
명 과목, 주제

subject   subject

subway

[sʌ́bwèi 섭웨이]
명 지하철

subway   subway   subway   subway

such

[sʌtʃ 서취]
형 그러한, 그런

such　such　such　such　such　such

sugar

[ʃúgər 슈거]
명 설탕

sugar　sugar　sugar

summer

[sʌ́mər 서머]
명 여름

summer　summer

sun

[sʌn 선]
명 태양

sun　sun　sun　sun　sun　sun　sun

Sunday

[sʌ́ndi 선디]
명 일요일

Sunday   Sunday

supermarket

[súːpərmàːrkit 수-퍼마-킷]
명 슈퍼마켓

supermarket   supermarket

supper

[sʌ́pər 서퍼]
명 만찬, 저녁식사

supper   supper   supper   supper

sure

[ʃuər 슈어]
형 확신하고 있는, 틀림없는

sure   sure   sure   sure

surprise

[sərpráiz 서프라이즈]
동 놀라다, 놀라게 하다

surprise   surprise

sweater

[swétər 스웨터]
명 스웨터

sweater   sweater   sweater   sweater

sweet

[swi:t 스위-트]
형 달콤한

sweet   sweet   sweet   sweet   sweet

swim

[swim 스윔]
동 수영하다

swim   swim   swim

T t

table [téib-əl 테이블] 몡 식탁

table   table   table   table   table

tail [teil 테일] 몡 꼬리

tail   tail   tail   tail

take [teik 테이크] 통 잡다

take   take   take   take   take   take

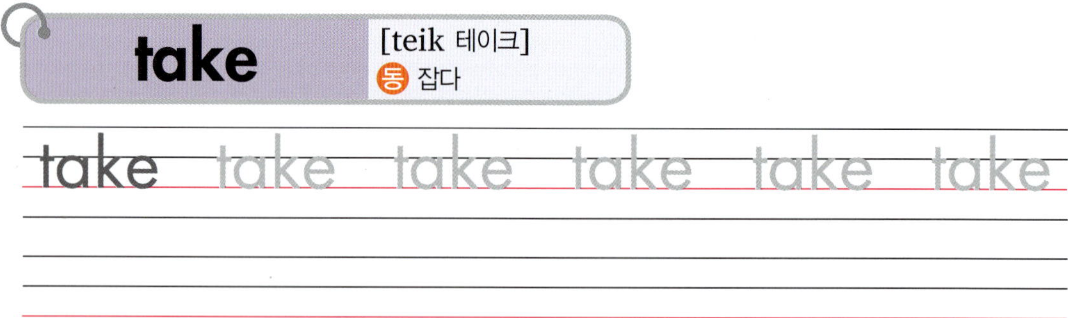

talk
[tɔːk 토-크]
동 말하다

talk talk talk talk talk talk talk

tall
[tɔːl 토-올]
형 키 큰

tall tall tall tall tall

tape
[teip 테이프]
명 테이프

tape tape tape tape tape tape

taste
[teist 테이스트]
명 맛, 미각

taste taste taste

taxi

[tǽksi 택시]
명 택시

taxi taxi taxi taxi

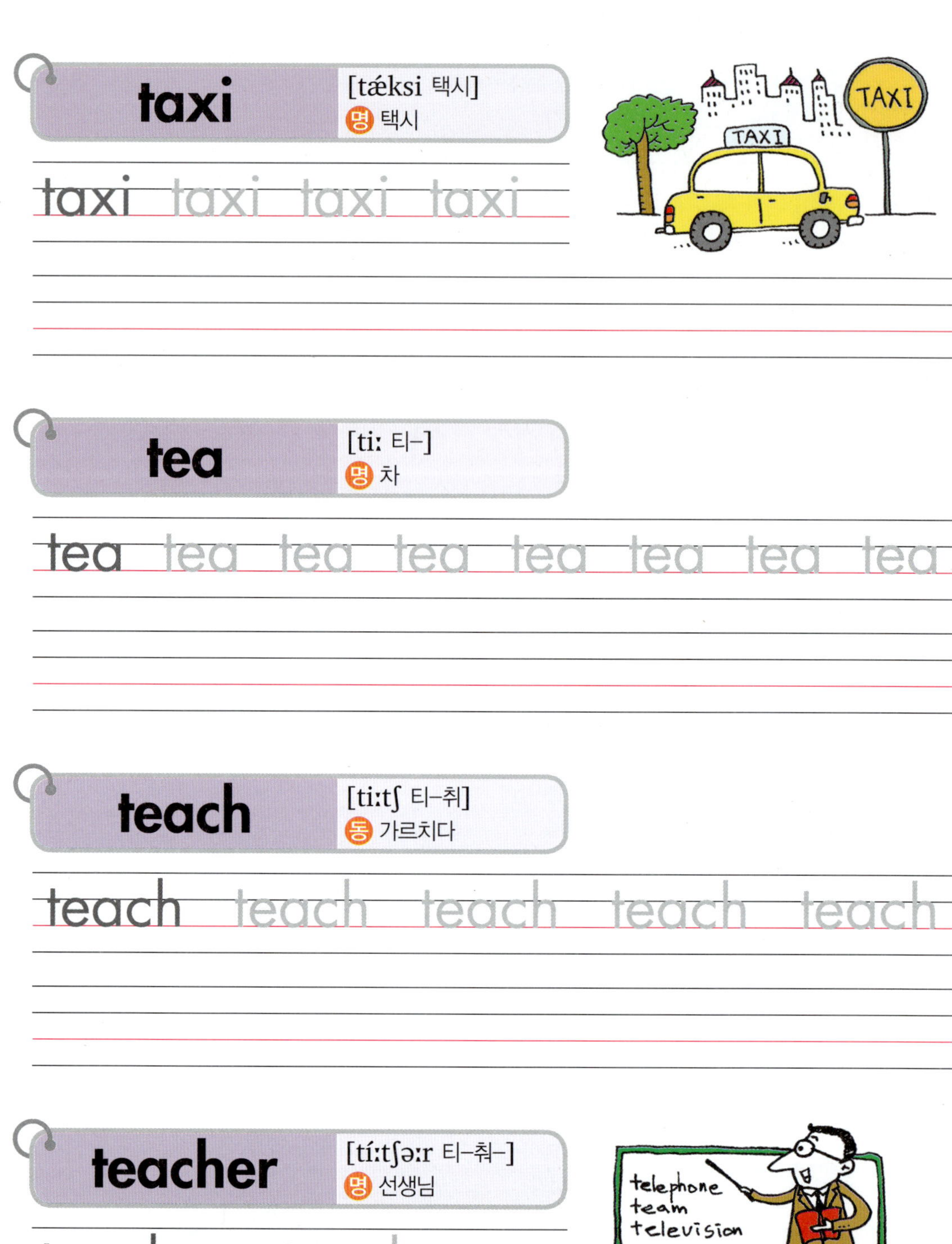

tea

[ti: 티-]
명 차

tea tea tea tea tea tea tea tea

teach

[ti:tʃ 티-취]
동 가르치다

teach teach teach teach teach

teacher

[tíːtʃəːr 티-춰-]
명 선생님

teacher teacher

team

[ti:m 티-임]
명 조, 팀

team team team

telephone

[téləfòun 텔러포운]
명 전화(기)

telephone telephone telephone

tell

[tel 텔]
동 말하다, 이야기하다

tell tell tell tell tell tell tell tell

television

[téləvìʒ-ən 텔러비전]
명 텔레비전

television television

ten

[ten 텐]
명 10, 열

ten ten ten ten ten

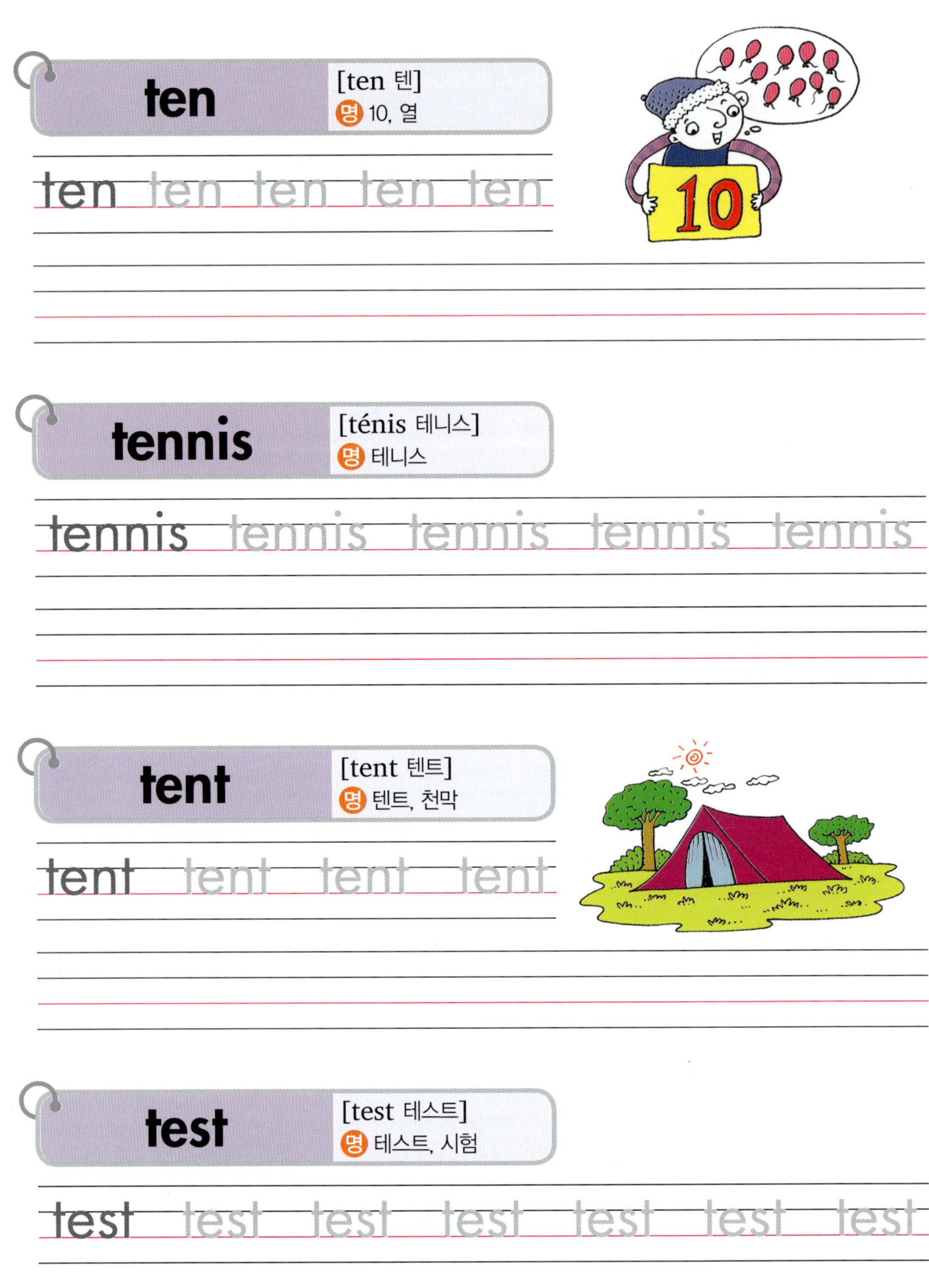

tennis

[ténis 테니스]
명 테니스

tennis tennis tennis tennis tennis

tent

[tent 텐트]
명 텐트, 천막

tent tent tent tent

test

[test 테스트]
명 테스트, 시험

test test test test test test test

textbook

[tékstbùk 텍스트북]
명 교과서

textbook textbook

than

[ðæn 댄]
접 ~보다

than than than than than than

thank

[θæŋk 쌩크]
동 감사하다

thank thank thank thank thank

that

[ðæt 댓]
대 저것

that that that that

theater

[θíətə:r 씨어터-]
명 극장

theater　　theater

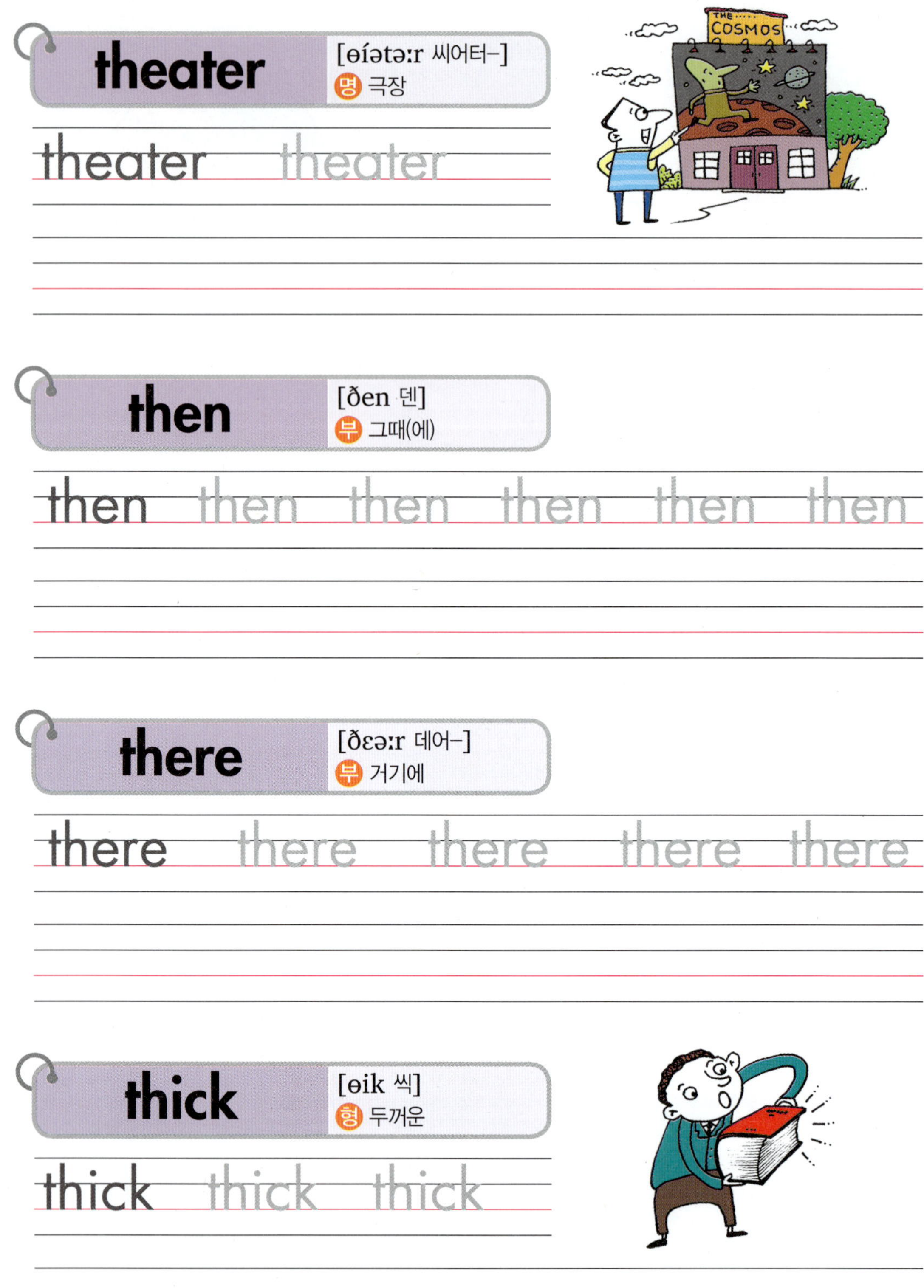

then

[ðen 덴]
부 그때(에)

then　then　then　then　then　then

there

[ðɛə:r 데어-]
부 거기에

there　there　there　there　there

thick

[θik 씩]
형 두꺼운

thick　thick　thick

thin

[θin 씬]
형 얇은

thin　thin　thin　thin

thing

[θiŋ 씽]
명 것, 물건

thing　thing　thing　thing　thing

think

[θiŋk 씽크]
동 생각하다

think　think　think

third

[θə:rd 써-드]
형 제 3의; 세(번)째의

third　third　third　third　third　third

thirteen

[θə̀ːrtíːn 써-티-인]
명 13, 열 셋

thirteen thirteen

thirty

[θə́ːrti 써-티]
명 30, 서른

thirty thirty thirty thirty thirty

this

[ðis 디스]
대 이것은(이)

this this this this

thousand

[θáuz-ənd 싸우전드]
명 1000, 천

thousand thousand thousand

three

[θri: 쓰리−]
명 3, 셋

three　three　three　three　three

through

[θru: 쓰루−]
전 ～을 통하여

through　through　through　through

throw

[θrou 쓰로우]
동 (내)던지다

throw　throw　throw

thumb

[θʌm 썸]
명 엄지손가락

thumb　thumb　thumb

Thursday
[θə́:rzdi 써-즈디]
명 목요일

Thursday   Thursday   Thursday

ticket
[tíkit 티킷]
명 표, 입장권

ticket ticket ticket ticket ticket

tie
[tai 타이]
동 묶다

tie tie tie tie tie

tiger
[táigə:r 타이거-]
명 호랑이

tiger tiger tiger

till

[til 틸]
전 ~까지

till till till till till till till till till till

time

[taim 타임]
명 시간

time time time time

tired

[taiə:rd 타이어–드]
형 피로한, 지친

tired tired tired

to

[tu: 투–]
전 ~로, ~에게

to to to to to to to to to to to to

today

[tədéi 터데이]
명 오늘

today today today today today

together

[təgéðəːr 터게더-]
부 함께

together together

tomato

[təméitou 터메이토우]
명 토마토

tomato tomato

tomorrow

[təmɔ́ːrou 터모-로우]
명 내일

tomorrow tomorrow tomorrow

tonight

[tənáit 터나이트]
명 오늘

tonight　tonight　tonight　tonight

too

[tu: 투-]
부 ~도(또한), 너무

too　too　too　too　too　too　too

tooth

[tu:θ 투-쓰]
명 이

tooth　tooth　tooth

top

[tap 탑]
명 정상, 꼭대기

top top top top top

touch

[tʌtʃ 터취]
동 만지다

touch　touch　touch

toward

[tɔːrd 토-드]
전 ~쪽으로

toward　toward　toward　toward

towel

[táu-əl 타우얼]
명 타월, 수건

towel　towel　towel

tower

[táuəːr 타우어-]
명 탑, 망루

tower　tower　tower　tower　tower

town

[taun 타운]
명 읍, (소)도시

town town town town town town

toy

[tɔi 토이]
명 장난감

toy toy toy toy

train

[trein 트레인]
명 열차

train train train train train train

travel

[træv-əl 트래벌]
동 여행하다

travel travel travel

tree

[tri: 트리-]
명 나무

tree tree tree tree

trip

[trip 트립]
명 여행

trip trip trip trip trip trip trip

trouble

[trʌb-əl 트러벌]
명 고생, 근심

trouble trouble

true

[tru: 트루-]
형 진실한

true true true true true true true

try

[trai 트라이]
동 시도하다, 노력하다

try try try try try try try try try

Tuesday

[tjúːzdi 튜-즈디]
명 화요일

Tuesday Tuesday Tuesday Tuesday

tulip

[tjúːlip 튜-울립]
명 튤립

tulip tulip tulip tulip

turn

[təːrn 터-언]
동 돌리다, 돌다

turn turn turn turn

turtle

[tə́:rtl 터–틀]
명 바다거북

turtle　turtle　turtle　turtle　turtle

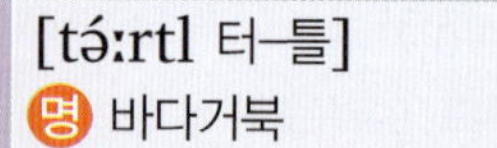

twelve

[twelv 트웰브]
명 12, 열 둘

twelve　twelve　twelve

twenty

[twénti 트웬티]
명 20, 스물

twenty　twenty　twenty　twenty

two

[tu: 투–]
명 2, 둘

two　two　two　two

276

type

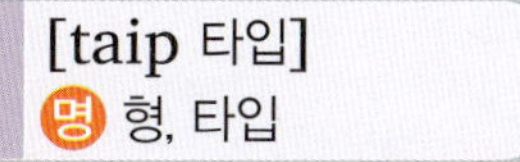

[taip 타입]
명 형, 타입

type type type type

Uu

ugly
[ˈʌgli 어글리]
형 추한, 못생긴

ugly　ugly　ugly　ugly　ugly　ugly

umbrella
[ʌmbrélə 엄브렐러]
명 우산

umbrella　umbrella

uncle
[ˈʌŋkəl 엉컬]
명 아저씨, 삼촌

uncle　uncle　uncle

under

[ʌ́ndər 언더]
전 ~아래에

under　under　under

understand

[ʌ̀ndərstǽnd 언더스탠드]
동 이해하다

understand understand understand

until

[əntíl 언틸]
전 ~까지

until until until until

up

[ʌp 업]
부 ~위로, 위에

up up up up up up up up up

upstairs

[ʌ́pstéərz 업스테어즈]
명 위층, 2층

upstairs　upstairs

us

[ʌs 어스]
대 우리를(에게)

us　us　us　us　us　us　us　us　us　us

use

[juːz 유-즈]
동 쓰다, 사용하다

use　use　use　use

useful

[júːsfəl 유-스펄]
형 쓸모 있는, 유용한

useful　useful　useful　useful　useful

usual

[júːʒuəl 유-주얼]
형 보통의, 일상의

usual　usual　usual　usual　usual

usually

[júːʒwəli 유-주월리]
부 보통

usually　usually

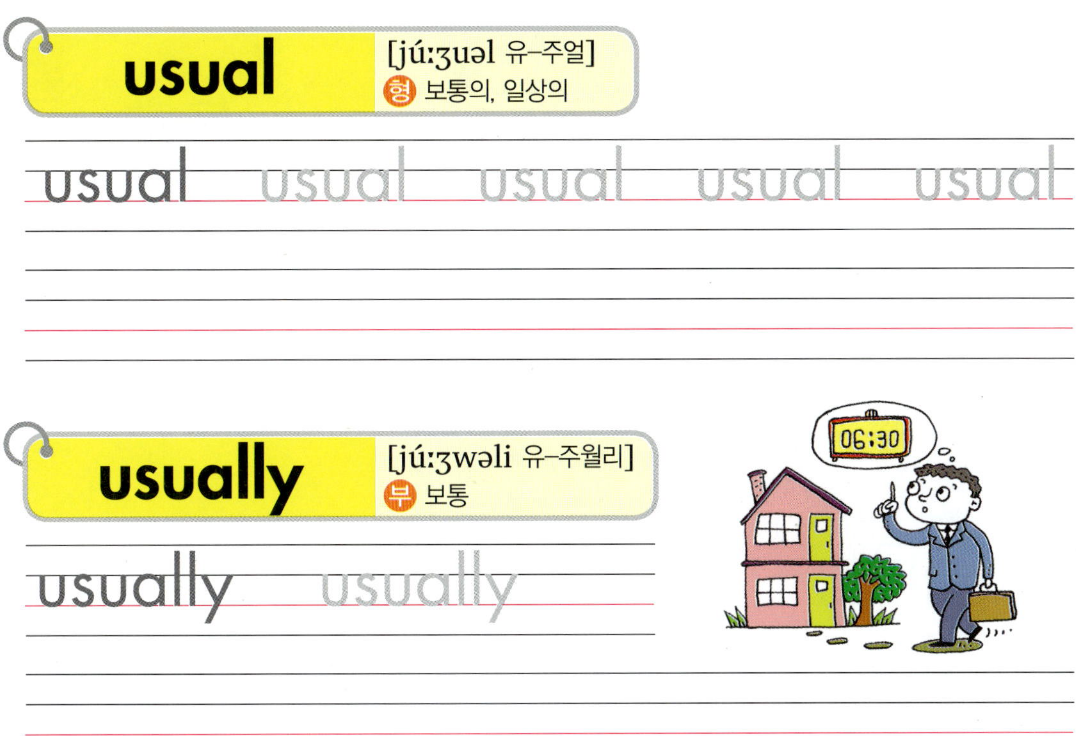

Vv

vacation
[veikéiʃən 베이케이션]
명 휴가

vacation　　vacation　　vacation

valley
[vǽli 밸리]
명 골짜기, 계곡

valley　valley　valley　valley　valley

vase
[veis 베이스]
명 (꽃)병

vase　vase　vase

vegetable

[védʒətəbəl 베줘터벌]
명 야채

vegetable　vegetable

very

[véri 베리]
부 대단히, 매우

very　very　very　very　very　very

video

[vídiòu 비디오우]
명 비디오, 영상

video　video　video　video　video

view

[vju: 뷰]
명 전망, 경치

view　view　view

village

[vílidʒ 빌리쥐]
명 마을

village   village

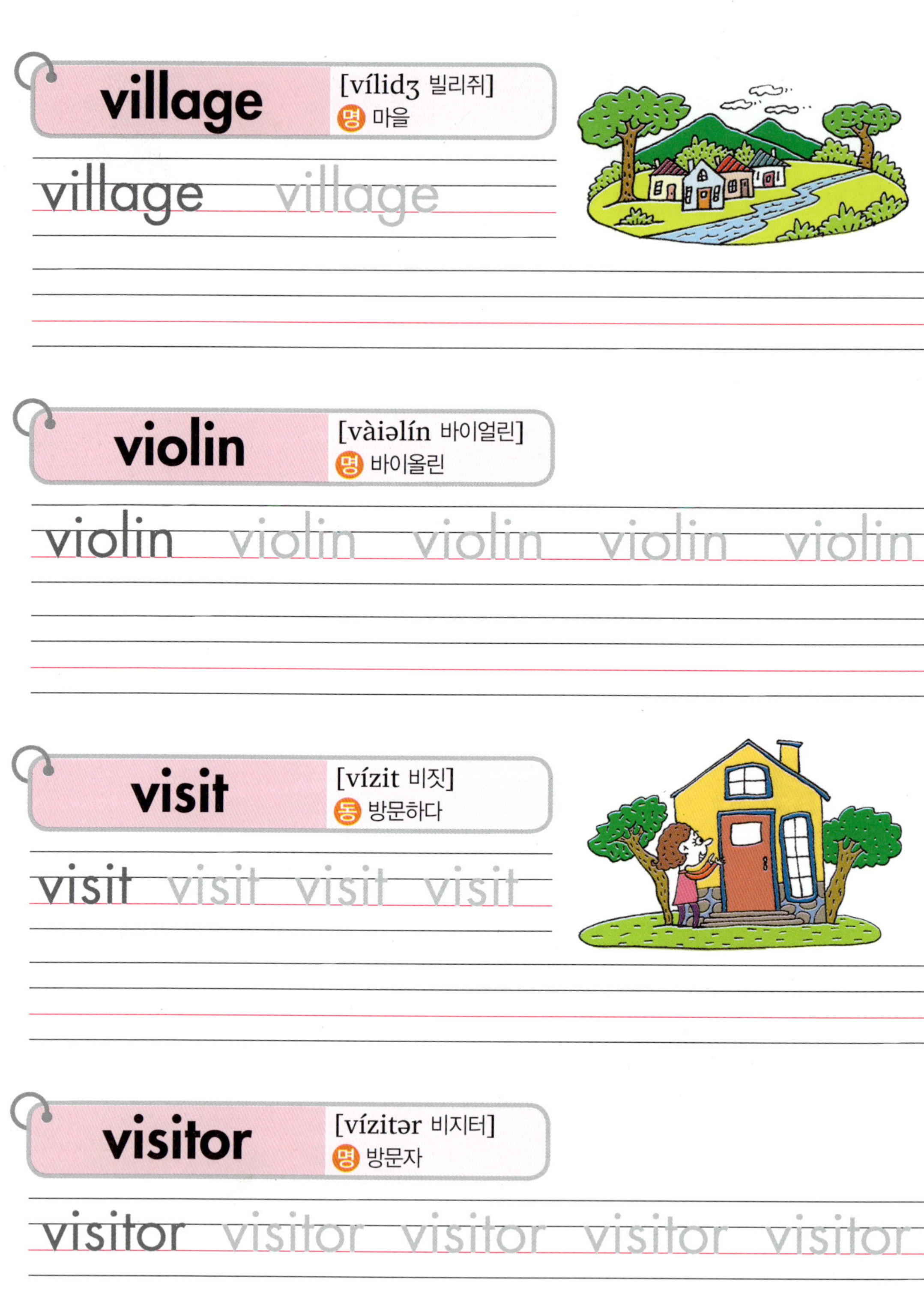

violin

[vàiəlín 바이얼린]
명 바이올린

violin   violin   violin   violin   violin

visit

[vízit 비짓]
동 방문하다

visit   visit   visit   visit

visitor

[vízitər 비지터]
명 방문자

visitor   visitor   visitor   visitor   visitor

voice

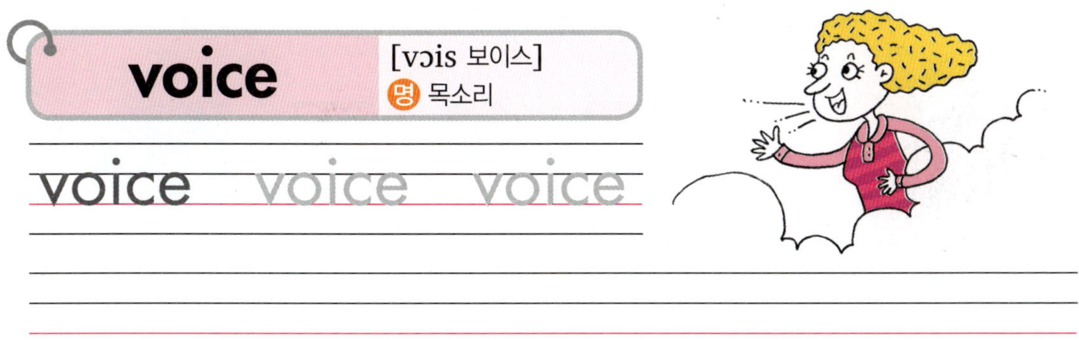

voice   voice   voice

W w

wait [weit 웨이트]
동 기다리다

wait   wait   wait   wait   wait   wait

wake [weik 웨이크]
동 잠깨다

wake   wake   wake

walk [wɔːk 워-크]
동 걷다

walk   walk   walk   walk   walk

wall

[wɔːl 워-얼]
명 벽, 담

wall wall wall wall

want

[wɔ(ː)nt 원트]
동 원하다

want want want want want

war

[wɔːr 워-]
명 전쟁, 싸움

war war war war war war

warm

[wɔːrm 워-엄]
형 따뜻한

warm warm warm

wash

[waʃ 와쉬]
동 씻다

wash　wash　wash

watch

[watʃ 와취]
동 지켜보다

watch　watch　watch　watch　watch

water

[wɔ́:tər 워-터-]
명 물

water　water　water

way

[wei 웨이]
명 길, 도로

way　way　way　way　way　way

wear

[wεəːr 웨어-]
동 입고 있다

wear　wear　wear

weather

[wéðəːr 웨더-]
명 일기, 기후

weather　weather

wedding

[wédiŋ 웨딩]
명 결혼식

wedding　wedding　wedding

Wednesday

[wénzdi 웬즈디]
명 수요일

Wednesday　Wednesday

week

[wi:k 위-크]
명 주, 일주일

week   week   week   week   week

weekend

[wíːkènd 위-켄드]
명 주말

weekend   weekend   weekend

welcome

[wélkəm 웰컴]
동 환영하다

welcome   welcome

well

[wel 웰]
부 잘, 능숙하게

well   well   well   well   well   well

 **west**

[west 웨스트]
명 서쪽

west   west   west   west   west   west

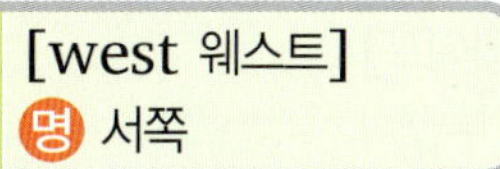 **while**

[hwail 와일]
접 ~하는 동안에

while   while   while

white

[hwait 와이트]
명 흰색

white   white   white   white   white

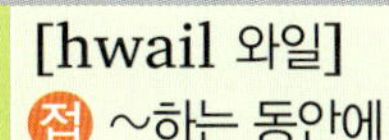 **wide**

[waid 와이드]
형 넓은

wide   wide   wide

wife

[waif 와이프]
명 아내, 부인

wife   wife   wife   wife   wife   wife

will

[wil 윌]
조 ~일(할) 것이다

will   will   will   will   will   will   will

win

[win 윈]
동 이기다

win   win   win   win

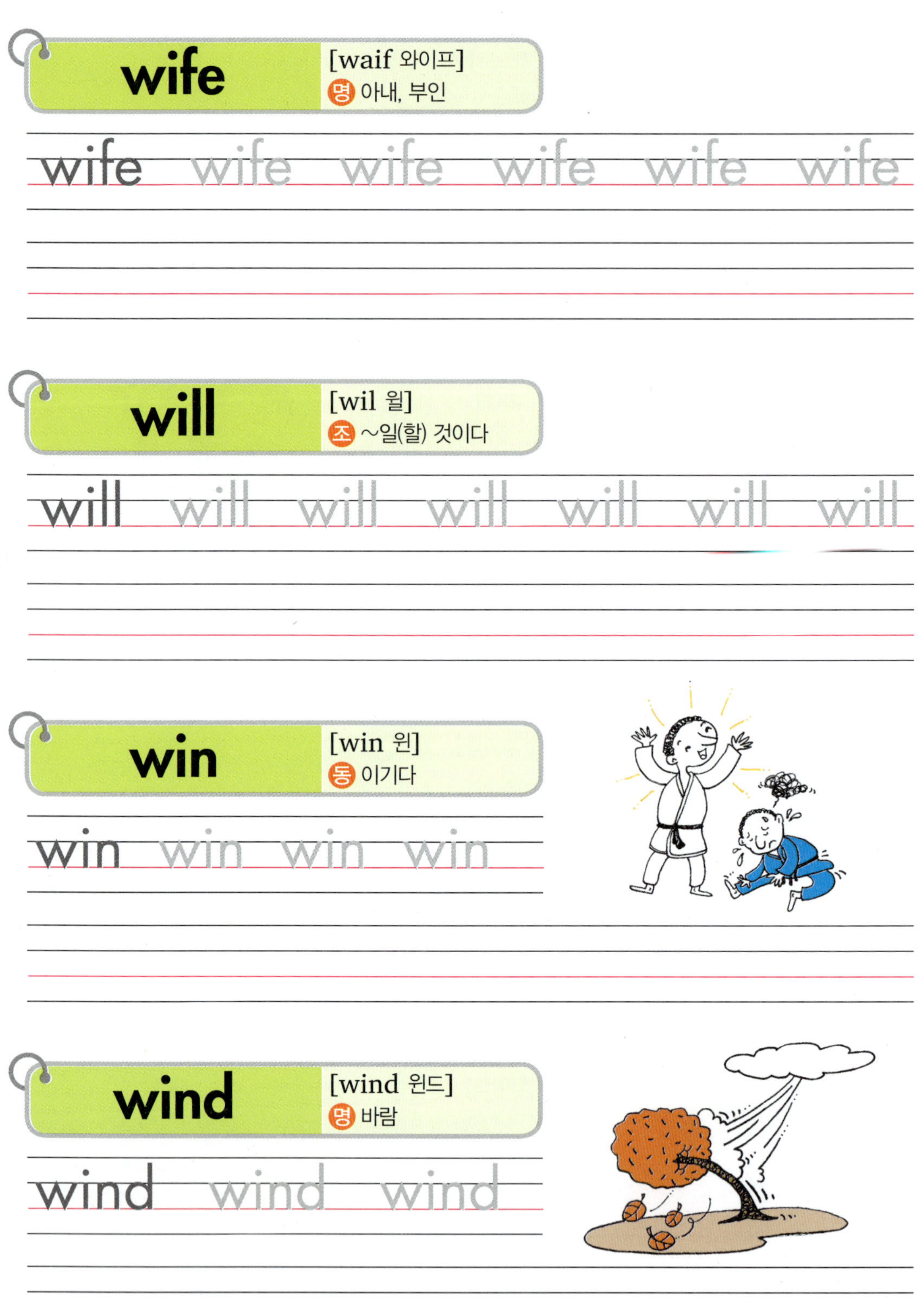

wind

[wind 윈드]
명 바람

wind   wind   wind

window
[wíndou 윈도우]
명 창문

window　window

windy
[windi 윈디]
형 바람이 센

windy windy windy windy windy

wing
[wiŋ 윙]
명 날개

wing wing wing wing wing wing

winter
[wíntəːr 윈터-]
명 겨울

winter winter winter

wise

[waiz 와이즈]
형 현명한, 슬기로운

wise wise wise wise wise wise

wish

[wiʃ 위쉬]
동 바라다, 원하다

wish wish wish

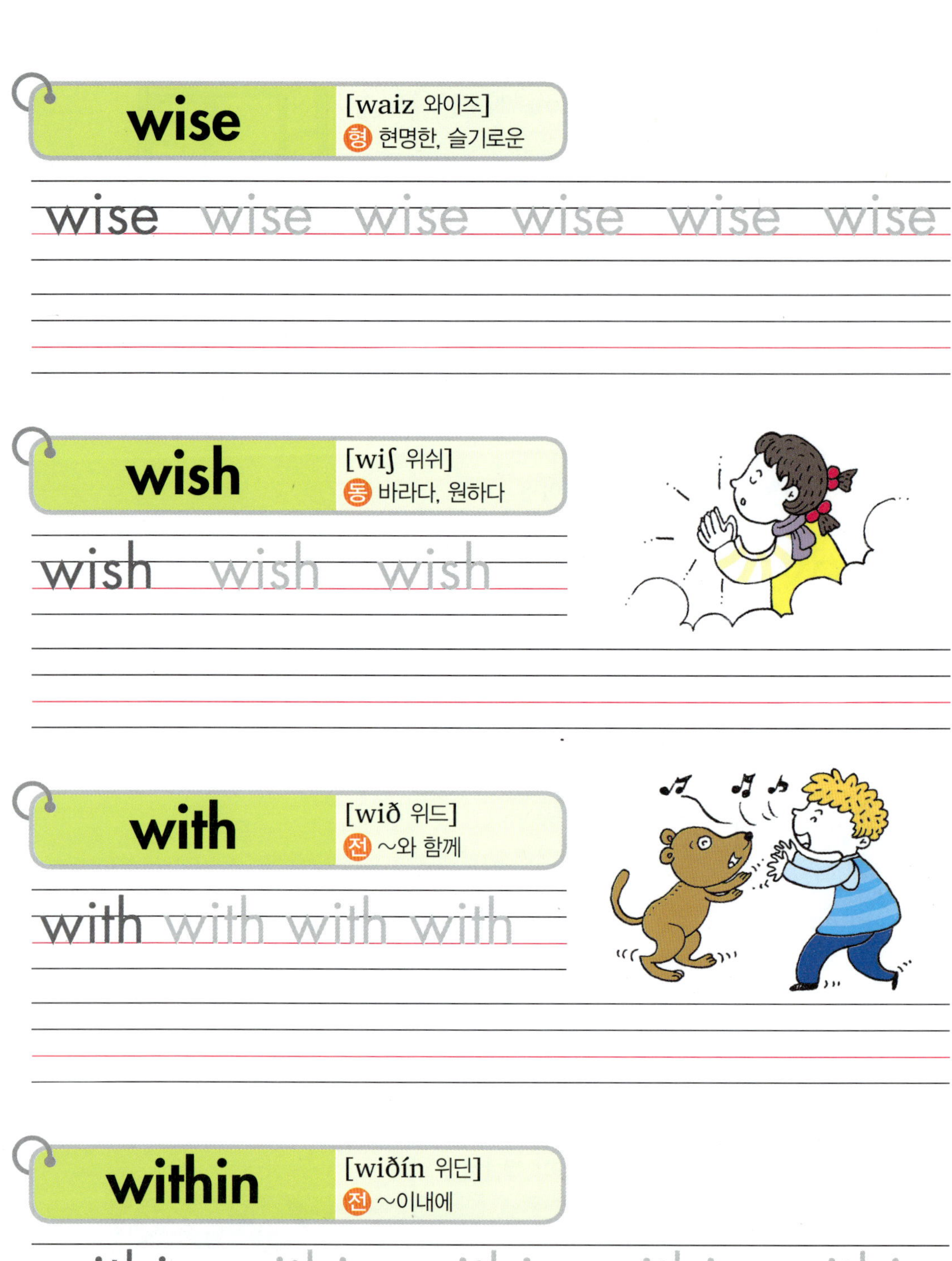

with

[wið 위드]
전 ～와 함께

with with with with

within

[wiðín 위딘]
전 ～이내에

within within within within within

without

[wiðáut 위다우트]
전 ~없이

without　without　without　without

wolf

[wulf 울프]
명 늑대

wolf wolf wolf wolf

woman

[wúmən 우먼]
명 여자

woman　woman　woman　woman

wonder

[wʌ́ndəːr 원더-]
동 궁금하다. 놀라다

wonder　wonder

wonderful

[wʌ́ndə:rfəl 원더-펄]
형 놀라운. 훌륭한

wonderful wonderful wonderful

wood

[wud 우드]
명 나무, 목재

wood wood wood

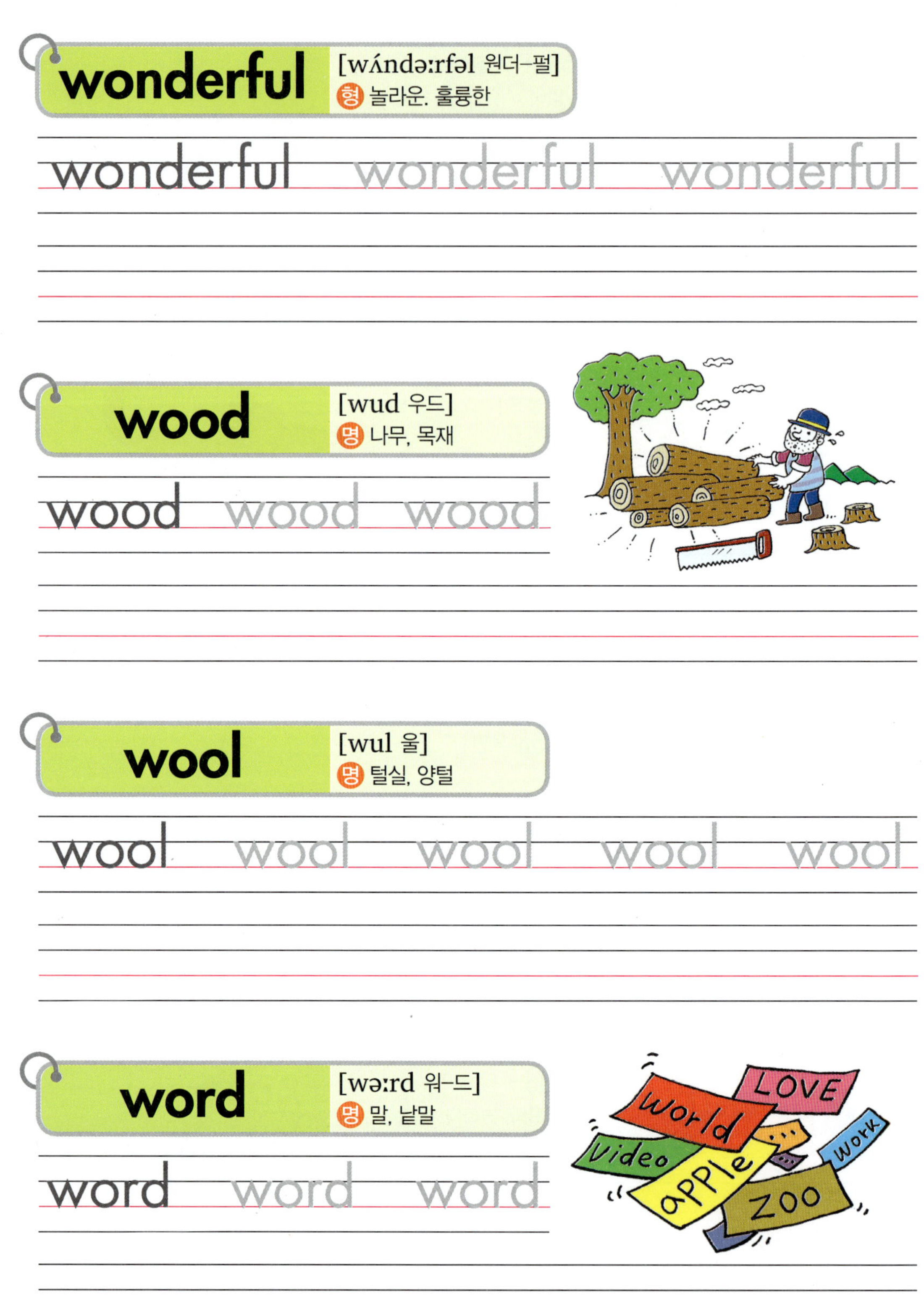

wool

[wul 울]
명 털실, 양털

wool wool wool wool wool

word

[wə:rd 워-드]
명 말, 낱말

word word word

work

[wə:rk 워-크]
명 일

work　work　work

world

[wə:rld 워-얼드]
명 세계, 세상

world　world　world　world　world

worry

[wə́:ri 워-리]
동 걱정하다

worry　worry　worry

would

[wud 우드]
조 ~일(할) 것이다

would　would　would　would　would

write

[rait 라이트]
동 쓰다

write write write write write write

wrong

[rɔːŋ 로-옹]
형 나쁜, 잘못된

wrong wrong wrong

d
f
B
i
w
e
P
Y
R
S
g
A

X x

X-ray

[éksrèi 엑스레이]
형 엑스선의

X-ray   X-ray   X-ray   X-ray   X-ray

xylophone

[záiləfòun 자일러포운]
명 실로폰, 목금

xylophone   xylophone

Yy

year

[jiə:r 이어–]

명 연(年), 해

year　year　year

yellow

[jélou 옐로우]

명 노랑

yellow　yellow　yellow　yellow

yes

[jes 예스]

명 예, 그래(긍정의 말)

yes　yes　yes　yes

yesterday

[[jéstə:rdi 예스터-디]
부 어제

yesterday   yesterday   yesterday

yet

[jet 옛]
부 아직

yet   yet   yet   yet   yet   yet   yet   yet

young

[jʌŋ 영]
형 젊은

young young young

Zz

---

zebra

[zíːbrə 지-브러]
명 얼룩말

zebra   zebra   zebra

---

zero

[zí-ərou 지-어로우]
명 제로, 영

zero   zero   zero

---

zoo

[zuː 주-]
명 동물원

zoo   zoo   zoo   zoo   zoo   zoo

F
A
B
z
M
R